ROBIN HOOD
A True Legend

SEAN McGLYNN

© Sean McGlynn 2018

Sean McGlynn has asserted his rights under the Copyright, Design and Patents Act, 1988, to be identified as the author of this work.

First published by Sharpe Books 2018.

ACKNOWLEDGEMENT

Many, many thanks to Maddy McGlynn.

ROBIN HOOD: A True Legend

Chapter One - THE LEGEND

Introduction

Few legends retain such a hold on popular imagination as the adventures of Robin Hood. Just the mention of the name will almost certainly evoke a picture of a vibrant and brave "outlaw" and an outstanding archer who, from his forest fastness, battles on behalf of the downtrodden and the oppressed in his quest for justice. Only King Arthur surpasses him in mythological status.

Such is his fame that around the globe different nations and cultures will often have their own equivalent of a Robin Hood in their mythologies, a figure fighting for fairness and helping the poor against corrupt rule. Invariably, these are known today as the "Robin Hood of India" (Tantia Bhil), the "Robin Hood of Provence" (Gaspard de Besse), the "Robin Hood of Germany" (Johannes Bückler), and so on. Very often, as with Tantia Bhil and Johannes Bückler, the figure is one fighting for independence from a foreign oppressor. This is an extremely important facet of the Robin Hood mythology which I believe will bring us closer to the real-life inspiration behind the legend.

Robin's quest for justice has already lasted for nearly a thousand years, from his medieval origins to present-day cultural manifestations on the screen, whether in TV's successful *Arrow* series, based on DC Comics' *Green Arrow* (which itself is an updating of the Robin Hood story) to yet another Hollywood remaking of the Robin Hood tale in 2018.

The purpose of this book is to delve into the medieval historical context that brought forth the Robin Hood legend and then to examine the reality behind the stories. What is surprising is that for such a mythical figure there is plenty of this reality to ponder on. Indeed, it is my contention here that writers on Robin Hood – be they historians, folklorists, literary scholars, etc – have, despite excellent studies, often either not made enough of some key facets of this medieval context or have missed important aspects of it altogether. As we shall see by the end of the book, these pieces can be joined together to offer an historical figure who I believe is the most significant real-life inspiration behind the Robin Hood fable.

As a medieval historian, I never set out to "discover" a real Robin Hood; indeed, he was for a long while a character of only peripheral interest to me. But a few years ago during my research into my primary area of medieval warfare, I came across a little-known historical figure whom I have been studying since: someone who seemed to fit the bill for the "real-life" Robin Hood; someone who most closely matched the criteria of a legendary bandit figure (and famous for such activity in own his lifetime), who fitted the time frame perfectly and who was explicitly a bowman who led a force of archers. Of equal importance, he neatly solves what I call the "hero/outlaw paradox". This hero/outlaw paradox of Robin Hood raises the question of how an infamous outlaw could also be a genuine hero at one and the same time. My chief candidate resolves this paradox.

Another key point which we shall explore is how surviving medieval tales of heroic characters, no matter how exaggerated and how fantastically and fictionally embellished with literary artifices, are often based on genuine historical figures, nebulous or otherwise, be they the Viking Ragnar Lothbrook or the hundreds of Christian saints, El Cid or the Robin Hood candidates Hereward the Wake, Fulk Fitzwarine and Eustace the Monk. Here fact, magic and moral didactics are all interwoven into the same thread.

Sidney Lee, the second editor of the authoritative *Dictionary of National Biography*, justified the inclusion of a "biography" of Robin Hood in this massive, multi-volume work on the grounds that he was one of eleven "legendary personages or creatures of romance who have been mistaken for heroes of history". Pollard echoes many views in stating that "Robin Hood is essentially a fictional creation". The consensus is that Robin is a compositional figure, rather than an historical figure. It is now time to examine the legend and to judge to what extent Robin Hood was the literary embodiment of a real-life medieval hero.

The Legend

It is remarkable how so much of the Robin Hood legend stems from so little. In effect, the whole mythology originates from a few mid and late fifteenth-century ballads and some later sixteenth-century renditions of the tale. These few sources, mainly literary, continue to fuel the Robin Hood industry in all its facets: film, literature, heritage, tourism and even in politics (with many today advocating a redistributive "Robin Hood tax").

The problem with these original sources is that they are already so dated and adapted by the time of their appearance that they cannot be considered as primary historical sources at all for Robin Hood, but rather should be considered as much later literary and artistic interpretations. As we shall see, Robin Hood was already a legendary figure by the mid-thirteenth century; so fifteenth-century representations are not much closer to the original figure than we are today to Dick Turpin from the early eighteenth century.

The earliest known Robin Hood tales appear in rhyming form from around 1450, surviving in a manuscript collection that appropriately enough includes a prayer of protection against outlaws.

"Robin Hood and the Monk" is a bloody and rather dark tale

in which the hero's role is played as much by Little John as by Robin Hood. The pair leave Sherwood Forest so that they may travel to Nottingham where Robin can hear mass. On the way they quarrel over their archery skills; Little John returns to Sherwood in a huff, while Robin continues on to the city. Here he is recognised and revealed by a monk (the monastic community rarely emerges well in a Robin Hood tale) and is arrested, after a fight in which Robin slays twelve of the Sheriff of Nottingham's men and breaks his sword on the Sheriff's head. Robin exclaims about his swordsmith: "I pray God to bring him woe!"

When Robin's men hear of his capture, Little John takes charge and seeks revenge against the monk; on finding him he "Struck off the monk's head". This is standard fare for a medieval tale, but more shocking is that John's companion also decapitates the monk's young page who is accompanying the monk. Little John and Much the Miller's Son, another of Robin's "Merry Men" band of outlaws, then rescue Robin, killing his gaoler and escaping over the walls of Nottingham castle.

"Robin Hood and Guy of Gisborne" may stem from the 1470s. It opens, as the tale of the Monk does, in the idyllic greenwood (this time situated in Barnsdale). Once again, Robin and Little John split from each other after an argument. Little John returns to the forest to find the outlaws' camp under attack, with two of his comrades killed and Will Scarlet in flight. Little John puts up a spirited resistance, killing one of the Sheriff's men, but is captured, tied to a tree, and will face execution "hanged high on a hill".

Meanwhile, Robin's encounter with a yeoman dressed in a horse's hide soon becomes violent; this not unsurprising given the nature of the Robin Hood tales and that Guy is a bounty hunter. Following the obligatory archery competition, the stranger announces himself to be Guy of Gisborne, while our hero reveals himself, tellingly, as "Robin Hood of Barnsdale". Of course, they proceed to have a real set-to in which Guy wounds Robin in the side with his sword. Robin manages to rally himself and kills Guy. The story then takes a particularly dark turn, and one in which Robin acts in a way unfamiliar and disturbing to modern audiences. He mutilates the face with "an Irish knife" and then "He took Sir Guy's head by the hair / And stuck it on the end of his bow". Disguised in Guy's hide, Robin makes his way to Barnsdale and tricks the Sheriff into releasing Little John as his reward for "killing Robin Hood". Realising his mistake, the Sheriff attempts to flee but is killed by "a broad arrow" let loose by John.

"Robin Hood and the Potter" comes from a manuscript dated 1503 and is altogether lighter in tone. (There is a reasonable argument to be made that the more violent the tale, the earlier its likely origins.) The "proud potter" is proceeding through the forest when he is waylaid by Robin and told to pay a toll to pass. The potter, a tough character, is having none of this and falls into a fight, using his staff to defeat Robin, who is wielding a sword and buckler. Mutual respect follows the combat.

Robin then takes on the disguise of the potter and enters the city of Nottingham where he makes a gift of some of his pots to the Sheriff's wife. In her gratitude, she invites Robin to dinner with the Sheriff. (As so often with the stories of Robin, the modern reader must overlook the implausibility of much of the content.) Unsurprisingly, Robin ends up in an archery contest, impresses the Sheriff and convinces him that he knows, and can lead him to, Robin Hood. Of course, Robin leads him straight into an ambush by his gang. The Sheriff is deprived of his horse and sent back shamefacedly to Nottingham.

"The Death of Robin Hood" (or "Robin Hood his Death") is possibly very early, from circa 1450. Like the Monk's tale, it is also incomplete. Robin declares his intention to visit the Cistercian Nunnery at Kirklees Priory to let some blood. His cousin is the prioress there. He ignores the warnings of one of his men, Will Scarlet, and arrives at the priory with Little John. Robin pays his cousin twenty pounds in gold but, when the letting has started, he realises he has been tricked, for his blood flows thinly. The weakened Robin is run through by a foe named Red Roger before he dispatches his assailant, leaving his corpse to be fed on by dogs. Robin then prepares his soul for death and gives burial instructions to Little John: "Set my bright sword at my head / My arrows at my feet / And lay my yew-bow by my side." Other versions include the famous scene where Robin shoots an arrow and tells Little John to bury him where it lands.

The tales are all rollicking adventures, containing narrow escapes, betrayal, disguises, light-hearted trickery and gratuitous violence. But our main source of the Robin Hood legend, *A Gest of Robin Hood*, is surprisingly lacklustre by comparison, with the above elements taking secondary place to what is predominantly a frankly rather dull tale of financial transactions.

A Gest of Robin Hood assembles extant tales of Robin from circa 1450 onwards and is generally considered to be an early form of the legend. Leading historians of the Robin Hood tradition such as Pollard, Ayton, Ohlgren and Maddicott all favour the first half of the fourteenth-century for the *Gest*'s origins; Holt believes its context points to the thirteenth century.

Its popularity can be gleaned from the five published editions to which it gave rise. Here various strands of the Robin Hood tales are gathered together to provide the focal origins of the legend. As one observer has noted, it is "the encyclopedia of the medieval Robin Hood". There is disagreement over how to define it, whether as a lengthy ballad or a short epic. Holt, one of the foremost authorities of the legends, calls it "in effect a minstrel's serial, designed to be recited at intervals". Its composer / compiler is thought by some to be a northerner, perhaps from Yorkshire; this makes good sense given its setting in Wentbridge and Barnsdale, with occasional forays into Nottingham and Sherwood. Comprising eight cantos ("fyttes") totalling 456 four-line stanzas, it can be summarised briefly as follows.

It begins, as always, in the forest; this time identified as Barnsdale. The story-teller commands us to give ear and listen to his account of the "good yeoman" Robin Hood, "a proud outlaw" unmatched for his courtesy. With him are the yeomen Little John, Will Scarlet and Much the Miller's Son. Robin insists that he will not dine unless with a guest. His men come across a knight passing through the forest on the way to Doncaster (he is later identified as Sir Richard at the Lee). When Robin demands that the knight pay for the sumptuous meal he enjoys (Robin's hospitality only extended so far), the knight begs poverty. A search by Little John reveals the truth of this declaration. The impoverished knight is heavily in debt, to the tune of £400, to the wealthy abbot of St Mary's in York. If he is unable to repay the sum he will lose his lands. Robin orders that this amount be loaned from his treasure chest to the knight and, generously, provides him with suitable clothing (for he is shabbily dressed) and a fine new horse. Little John measures out the cloth with his bow stave. The loan is to be repaid a year hence.

The knight then heads to York to pay off the loan. Here the monks are portrayed as gleefully expecting the knight not to turn up for the payment deadline, and greedily pondering on the financial windfall they expect that day: "And we shall have to spend in this place / Four hundred pounds". But the knight does turn up. He eggs them on by pretending he does not have the money and is called a "false knight" by the abbot. The knight then relishes in handing over the money. He returns home and, over the year, gathers the money he owes to Robin Hood. In gratitude, he additionally collects for Robin one hundred sheaves of good arrows, each forty-five inches long and fletched with peacock feathers.

The *Gest* then reveals its compositional nature by starting another plotline in which Little John is the main character. The setting shifts to Nottingham for – what else? – an archery competition. Such is his skill he manages to split the target wand three times. (An historian has suggested that this has phallic connotations, an idea best not dwelt upon.)

Suitably impressed, the Sheriff of Nottingham offers John employment: "This man is the best archer that I have ever seen". John, who identifies himself with the appropriate alias of Reynold Greenleaf, accepts the offer, vowing to be a pain in the Sheriff's side: "I shall be the worst servant to him / That he ever had". Looking for food in the Sheriff's kitchen, John falls into an epic hour-long fight with the cook. Neither yield until John, appreciative of the cook's combative abilities, offers him paid employment in Robin Hood's gang. They abscond back to the forest with much of the Sheriff's silverware and over £300.

Later John, still under the pretence of being Greenleaf, entices the Sheriff to enter the forest in order to hunt a herd of 140 deer, promising him over sixty sharp anglers (he is referring to Robin's men and their arrows; the size of Robin's retinue is repeatedly given in the *Gest* as 140). The ensnared Sheriff, more benign than menacing here, ends up in Robin's camp, eating dinner off his own silver and stripped of his finery. After some humiliation, he is allowed to return to Nottingham.

The story now moves to its fourth canto in which a monk from St Mary's traveling through the forest is brought to Robin after the churchman's fifty-two strong guard take to their heels at the sight of Robin Hood's gang. The monk is not impressed to meet Robin (at his house, it is worth noting), whom he considers a "common thief". The monk is unchivalrous and displays bad manners over dinner, unlike the courteous and contrastingly chivalrous criminal. When the monk attempts to conceal the fact that he is carrying £800, Robin relieves him of the money, cheekily saying that the sum will cover the cost of dinner. Sending the monk packing, he requests that the abbot of St Mary's "send me such a monk / To dinner every day". At this juncture, the indebted knight, Sir Richard at the Lee, returns to repay Robin's loan. Flush with cash from the monk, Robin, in a typical act of generosity, not only allows the knight to keep the money, but gives him another £400 also.

Canto five introduces a more dramatic story, set around another archery contest, arranged by the Sheriff for "all the best archers of the North". Robin cannot resist the challenge and heads to Nottingham with his men to participate. Here he splits the target wand three times in a row; his men Gilbert with the White Hand, Little John, Will Scarlet and Much the Miller's Son also acquit themselves well. (The writer also names Reynold Greenleaf among Robin's men, perhaps a likely confusion between him and Little John that arises from the gathering together of various tales; it is just one of many inconsistencies in the *Gest*.)

Unsurprisingly, the contest is cover for an ambush. In the ensuing *mêlée* Little John is wounded by an arrow in the knee and pleads to Robin not to let the Sheriff capture him alive.

Heroically, Much carries John on his back, occasionally placing him on the ground to shoot his bow at the enemy. The outlaws find refuge in the castle of Sir Richard at the Lee.

In canto six the Sheriff arrives with the local militia and lays siege to the castle, calling Sir Richard a traitor. The knight responds by saying that he will await the king's resolution of the matter. King Edward affirms that he will travel north. (Which one we do not know, but it could be any from Edward I to, possibly, Edward IV if the *Gest* is compiled as late as 1460.) Meanwhile, Robin makes his way back to the forest, much to the vexation of the Sheriff. However, he is compensated by the capture of Sir Richard when the knight was out hawking. His wife appeals to Robin for help in preventing her husband from being "shamefully slain". Robin responds swiftly, leading his "seven score" men to Nottingham where (surprisingly) they are able to walk through the streets and meet up with the Sheriff. Robin bends "a full good bow" and lets loose an arrow that fells the Sheriff. Before he can regain his feet, Robin swings his sword to strike "off the Sheriff's head". Robin's men also "drew their bright swords / That were so sharp and keen / And laid into the Sheriff's men". Sir Richard is rescued and escapes with the outlaws to the forest.

Canto seven sees King Edward and his armed force arrive in Nottingham to capture Sir Richard and, hopefully, Robin Hood. In vain, he stays in the North for over six months, while Robin continues to deplete the king's deer herds. A plan is hatched for the king and five knights to enter the forest disguised as monks in a successful endeavour to lure out Robin and his men, who accost him on the road. Robin addresses the "abbot" (the disguise of the king) and demands money from the wealthy church. The king pleads (relative) poverty, handing over only £40. The courteous Robin gives half to "his merry men" and returns the other half to Edward. The "abbot" says that he is on the king's business and proves this by the display of the royal seal. Robin kneels before him avowing "I love no man in all the world / So well as I do my king". The king bids him to come and dine with him in Nottingham. Robin blows his large horn to summon all his 140 men and prepare a feast for the "abbot" and his men, consisting of "fat venison / Good white bread, good red wine / And fine brown ale".

As part of the entertainment an archery contest is arranged. At first the king is fearful that this means he will be killed, but his mind is soon put at rest. Two targets are set with a rose garland. Robin promises that any man who misses the garland will lose his gear and receive a clout around the head. He duly administers blows to Little John and Scarlet; when he himself misses, the "abbot" does the honours, knocking a surprised Robin to the ground. "'By God", said Robin, / "You are a stalwart friar'". Recognition dawns on Robin and he kneels before his king, as does Sir Richard at the Lee. All is settled amicably, with Robin and his now 143 men joining the king' service.

The final canto continues directly on from the previous one, with the king buying and donning an outfit of Lincoln green. They head for Nottingham, king and all dressed as "outlaws". There is laddish banter along the way as they play the archery game of "pluck-buffet", with even the king receiving a wallop from Robin for each time he misses a target. In the city, Sir Richard receives back all his land. Robin then spends fifteen months in the king's service during which time he spends a fortune on sustaining his retinue of knights and squires in order to maintain his "great renown". Of his men, only Little John and Will Scarlet remain with him. He laments his poverty and becomes nostalgic for the old days in the forest:

> "Alas!" said the good Robin,
> "My wealth is all gone away.
> I used to be a good archer,
> Solid and also strong.
> I was reckoned the best archer
> That was in Merry England."
> "Alas!" then said the good Robin,
> "Alas and well away!
> If I dwell longer with the king,
> My sorrow will me slay."

He asks the king's leave to return to Barnsdale for a week to build a chapel dedicated to Mary Magdalene. This is granted. Robin is again enchanted by his idyllic forest. Here he kills a large hart and blows his horn; and once more 140 men hurry to his side.

Ignoring both his word to Edward and the king's command to return after seven days, Robin remains there for the next twenty-two years. The tale then ends with Robin going to Kirklees to have his blood let there. Here he is tricked by his kinswoman the prioress of Kirklees. With her lover Sir Roger of Doncaster she betrays Robin (but we are not told how he meets his end). The *Gest* finishes with the only early reference to Robin helping the poor: "For he was a good outlaw / And did poor men much good."

This, then, is the main source of the Robin Hood legend. It is a charming, occasionally brutal tale. It is full of inconsistencies that point to its assembled nature – as do the characters that inhabit the story.

The Merry Men, a Marian Woman and an Arch Enemy

The earliest stories summarised above contain those well-known Merry Men Little John, Will Scarlet and Much the Miller's Son. However, it is doubtful that all were present at the birth of the legend.

Much of the time, Little John looms larger in the story than Robin himself; he certainly comes across as a vivid character, and almost equal to Robin in literary stature, appearing in all of the earliest ballads and a mainstay thereafter. A constant companion to Robin in his adventures and shared dangers, he is loyal but also of sufficient independence and character to stand up to Robin and argue with him. The relationship with Robin goes beyond service and loyalty to an obvious mutual respect and friendship. The name is likely a criminal alias, certainly a sobriquet, of the sort recorded in 1313 in Kent where one John of Shorne, charged with homicide, is known as "Petit Jehan" – Little John. Perceived as a real character, he also appears alongside Robin in four late medieval chronicles from Scotland, including Andrew of Wyntoun's *Original Chronicle* from circa 1420, in which the outlaws appear under the year 1283.

Will Scarlet (sometimes rendered Scathlock or Scathlok and numerous variations) is also present from the start. He plays an active, often heroic, but largely silent role in the stories and is clearly a loyal follower of Robin. However, though important enough to be named as a character, unlike John he is not a mainstay in future renditions of the tale. The surname Scathelock, Schathelok and Schathelok is recognisable in the fourteenth century, and may have its origins in Old English. Our earliest recording of the name goes back to 1196. Then again, Scarlet can suggest a connection to the Old French *escarlate*, denoting colour. Unsurprisingly, there is disagreement over the literal meaning of the name.

Interestingly, at one point in the *Gest*, Robin's men are kitted out in scarlet cloth and this offers a possible clothier association to Will. (Later the band reverts to Lincoln green, which seems an altogether more sensible mode of dress for outlaws attempting to hide in the forest.)

Although today less familiar than Will Scarlet, Much the Miller's Son has a much more prominent role in the first renditions of the Robin Hood legend, and is given lines to speak. The nickname Much does not tell us much about him; the Miller's Son offers a little more, if only that it suggests a reasonably comfortable financial background for his family. A character present from the start, he is not hesitant about launching into disturbingly violent episodes: in "Robin Hood and the Monk", while Little John beheads the monk, it is Much who dispatches the young page boy in similar fashion. In the *Gest* he is ever-present in Robin's adventures, heroically rescuing Little John when he is wounded in Nottingham.

What of the other characters so familiar from the Robin Hood stories? They come later. The troubadour Alan à Dale has to wait until the seventeenth century to make his debut appearance. There is a lot more substance to Friar Tuck, the rotund and jovial chaplain of the Merry Men. He first comes to light in the Robin Hood story around 1475, after the *Gest*, in both a ballad called "Robin Hood and the Curtal Friar" and the earliest Robin Hood play *Robin Hood and the Sheriff of Nottingham.*(A curtal friar, sometimes known as a kirtled friar, is one who wears a traveling habit.) As with Mary, the friar has associations with the May Day celebrations.

There is much said to be for Friar Tuck being based on a real-life figure. In 1416 and 1417, a royal writ was issued twice for the capture of a gang leader going under the *nom de guerre* of Friar Tuck. His armed gang was causing havoc in the forests and parks of Sussex and Surrey; game was stolen and the dwellings of foresters and warreners (servants of the crown) burned down. In 1417 a parliamentary petition had raised the urgent issue of armed bands breaking the law in this area. The friar was never caught, but his name was revealed in a pardon of 1429 as Robert Stafford, a chaplain of Sussex. We shall encounter the decidedly non-jovial Stafford again in the chapter on crime.

Two further points are worth noting here regarding the name. The first is that in 1417, the scribes of the writ comments on "the unusual name, in common parlance, of Frere Tuk". This clearly indicates the novelty of the name. Secondly, in regards to placing Robin Hood in his original time setting (if such he ever had), friars did not establish themselves in England until the 1220s. It is likely, then, that Friar Tuck was a late medieval addition to the legend.

Maid Marian also comes to the tales later, being first mentioned, alongside Robin, in Alexander Barclay's *Ship of Fools* from 1508 and in the 1509 Kingston Robin Hood play. She is not a part of the earliest ballads. The *Ship of Fools* seems to suggest that Marian belonged to her own separate story tradition: "Yet would I gladly hear some merry fytte [verse] / Of Maid Maid Marian, or else of Robin Hood." Beyond the names themselves, there is little to link the English Robin and Marian romance to that found in the French pastoral poem of the thirteenth-century, musically dramatized circa 1283 as *Robin et Marion* (or, *Le Jeu de Robin et Marion*). Here Robin is an ordinary peasant and Marion a shepherdess.

The character of Marian owes a debt to late medieval May Games celebrations. In these events, by the sixteenth century, Robin is often represented as the king and Marian as the queen of misrule. And misrule it often was: the authorities repeatedly tried to suppress the cider and ale driven antics of boisterous and ribald peasants taking full advantage of the licence to revel in the short-lived disorder and overthrow of the ruling hierarchy. Marian seems to have had her own separation tradition in these games at first, before becoming Robin Hood's lady.

Even Henry VIII got in on the act in the act with his queen, Catherine, during the court's 1515 Maying. As they rode to Shooters Hill they encountered "a company of tall yeomen, clothed all in green with green hoods and bows and arrows, to the number of 200". They were led, of course, by "Robin Hood", who invited the royal couple to breakfast on wine and venison in a specially arranged bower in the woods.

Robin Hood plays were frequently performed as part of the May Games in mid-fifteenth-century England and to the end of the sixteenth century (the earliest known reference for a Robin Hood play dates to 1426). It is likely that Robin Hood and Maid Marian (and Friar Tuck, as well) were better known through these May Games pageants and plays than through ballads and printed text. The perennial Robin Hood pantomime has a very long tradition.

As for Robin's arch enemy, the Sheriff of Nottingham, a number of issues arrive as to authenticity. The great majority of historians and folklorists place the origins of the Robin Hood legend between the late twelfth and early fourteenth centuries. However, the title of Sheriff of Nottingham did not exist until the mid-fifteenth century – the time from which the surviving ballads exist. Before this there existed the ancient office of shire-reeve and, post-conquest, High Sheriff of Nottinghamshire and Derbyshire. High Sheriffs exercised fiscal and judicial responsibilities on behalf of the king for their counties, so such a sheriff would indeed have been charged with the apprehending of criminals like Robin Hood. However, by the fifteenth century the office had lost importance. The role of the mid-fifteenth Sheriff of Nottingham was restricted mainly to municipal duties. Depending on which point of time is chosen for the origins of the Robin Hood stories, any number of candidates can be proffered as the real-life Sheriff of Nottingham. The point in the stories is that the Sheriff (never given a name) represents both oppressive taxation and especially a corrupt judicial system. He is the script's "bad guy". Robin's enduring role, from that time to this, has been to fight such injustice and mete out approved justice of his own.

All these characters share a long afterlife to the present day in the Robin Hood legends. But in reality, they probably have next to nothing to offer for those searching for the factual origins of Robin. As already alluded to above, the most famous characters – Maid Marian, Friar Tuck and probably Little John – are all likely to have originated in stories of their own. This helps to explain Little John's prominence in the earliest ballads, and the later introductions of Tuck and Marian as leading figures. Ballads of these may well have been contemporaneous with the Robin ones; if so, the lack of surviving written evidence is not surprising given the medium of oral tradition.

The fusing of different characters with their own separate traditions in this manner was a common medieval practice. A modern way to understand this is to consider the remarkable ongoing cinematic successes of American comic book superheroes. In 1963 Marvel Comics initiated the Avenger series by bringing together ("Avengers assemble!") a group of superheroes who were already established in their own comics: Thor, Iron Man, Ant Man and the Incredible Hulk. The Avengers' line-up itself varied over time, bringing in another established superhero almost immediately (Captain America, when the Hulk went solo) and then undergoing more cast changes than *Coronation Street*. Marvel was responding to a similar strategy by DC Comics, who in 1960 had brought together Superman, Batman and Wonder Woman to form the super-group The Justice League.

The crucial point here is that popular stories and characters are adapted over time to find new audiences and to stay relevant. Any number of literary or popular cultural figures, either from the distant or more recent past, go through these evolutions and transformations: Sherlock Holmes, Doctor Who, the Three Musketeers, etc. Robin Hood and his band of Merry Men are no different. Thus Robin Hood undergoes some heady social-climbing from a medieval yeoman in the 1450s to the Earl of Huntingdon by the end of the sixteenth century. If the Robin Hood legend was circulating in the early 1200s, it is likely to have evolved into something quite different more than two centuries later by the time of the earliest surviving ballads. Thus the question should be asked: what were the audiences of Robin Hood plays and ballads after?

Robin Hood's Medieval Audience

The most relevant answer to the above question is: entertainment. The Robin Hood stories can be interpreted in a number of ways, but we should give pride of place to their entertainment factor. Medieval people were no different to modern ones in seeking diversions from the hardships and tedium of everyday life through escapist adventures. The Robin Hood ballads offer action, violence, comedy and (mostly) a happy ending. The Robin Hood performances also offered comical coarseness: an official in Henry VIII's time complained about "the plays of Robin Hood, Maid Marian and

Friar Tuck, in which lewdness and ribaldry is placed in front of the people".

Audiences would also have appreciated the righteous violence dished out by Robin against deserving malefactors (although we must allow for shocking exceptions such as the innocent page boy in "Robin Hood and the Monk"). While righteous characters such as Sir Richard at the Lee emerge triumphant – and richer – from their travails, the likes of the Sheriff of Nottingham and Guy of Gisborne receive their fair dues in the form of violent death. Revenge has always been prevalent in literature and popular culture from Sophocles' Elektra to Charles Bronson in the *Death Wish* film series (starting in 1974 but reimagined once again in 2018 with Bruce Willis in the main role of the vigilante Paul Kersey – an observation I labour to re-emphasise my point above about reinventions of popular stories and characters). The ordinary person's quest for justice, rough or otherwise, was especially widespread in fifteenth-century England, as we shall see in the chapter on medieval crime, when attitudes to popular punishments would make Mr Kersey's views resemble those of liberal reformer rather than of an avenging vigilante.

Violence is central to the Robin Hood stories – as it is to so many medieval tales. Apart from the sempiternal allure of gratuitous violence in entertainment throughout the ages, the chivalric atmosphere of the medieval period encouraged a glorification of extreme martial acts, in which the heroic knight demonstrates his masculine probity by using his sword to cleave opponents in two from head to saddle. The *chansons de geste*, or songs of deeds, was the main outlet for this tradition of righteous violence, in which the brave knight wields his sword in vengeance, or for honour or for some great cause, often dying in the process. A few examples will give a flavour of these.

The hauberk proved no stronger than the straw:
From front to rear he rammed his lance's point
And flung him down to die in his gore
(*Raoul de Cambrai*)

The heathen's hand was smitten off, his eye
Plucked out, and then his nose half-split and sliced
(*Knights of Narbonne*)

He splits the skull, he dashes out the brains,
Down to the beard he cleaves him through the face
(*Song of Roland*)

Such explicit violence also populates works that marry deeds with genuine recorded history. That the Albigensian Crusade in Southern France has earned a reputation for extreme brutality is not surprising after this account written by a participant: "Sharp steel met flesh: noses, scalps and chins, arms, legs and feet, guts, livers and kidney lay strewn on the ground in lumps and gobbets" (from *Song of the Cathar Wars*).

The clergy were hardly any less blood-thirsty. William the Breton, a thirteenth-century royal chaplain in France, wrote of a military engagement in which eyes, hands, feet and ears are lost by many victims; throats are cut; stones crush skulls, axes shatter knee caps and clubs spatter brains. One man is engulfed in boiling tar and another sees his intestines hanging from his stomach.

While these excerpts come from the High Middle Ages when the *chansons* were at their most popular, their influence remained strong in the fifteenth century. The Deeds *of Don Pero Nino* from the 1430s tells of the hero fighting with a crossbow bolt sticking though his nose, which his opponents deliberately struck so as to make him "suffer great pain"; one enemy soldier "hit a great blow on the bolt with his shield and drove it further into his head". Don Pero dispatches another foe by splitting "his head down to the eyes". It is a story in which "blood is flowing abundantly in many places".

This preoccupation with violence borders on the psychotic in the poetry of the troubadour Bertrand de Born, someone who believes that "there is too much peace about". He writes of longing for Spring so that war can resume in earnest and he can once again "see the dead with lances piercing their sides".

Against this background, the violence in Robin Hood does not seem quite so shocking. Instead for its audiences it is both didactic and entertaining – and also perhaps a little titillating.

There are repeated clear elements of chivalry in the Robin Hood ballads. Robin is clearly courteous in the true, generous chivalric sense. He also carries – and uses – a sword, the ultimate symbol of true chivalry. Some leading historians such as Holt believe that the tales are designed for an audience of household retainers, knights and landed gentry; as we have seen with the Maying of Henry VIII, the highest in the land were familiar with the Robin Hood legends and happy to play along with them. Others such as Hilton favour an audience of peasant yeomanry. Dobson and Taylor opt for the new social group of prosperous yeomanry: landed, or craftsmen, property owners, businessmen – in effect, the middle classes. The *Gest* opens by addressing its audience as "gentlemen" "of freeborn blood", also denoting the middling sorts.

Robin's courtesy, manners and sword-play promote strong chivalric elements. In the *Gest* the word "courtesy" is deployed seventeen times; Robin comes to the aid of Sir Richard at the Lee's wife; Robin is deferential to those higher in the social hierarchy (if deserving); and Robin is generous to his men and others. Nonetheless, he is clearly portrayed as a "good yeoman" and the appeal amongst this growing class must be obvious. Certainly, those of yeomanry social status would have delighted in the fact that a fellow yeoman, Robin, could help a knight out of his financial distress and, what's more, could do so to the extent of £400 (ill-gotten gains aside).

The most persuasive position is perhaps held by Ohlgren. Building on earlier work done by Nerlich who argued for a new mind-set shifting "from the courtly-knightly ideology adventure to mercantile self-awareness and self-fashioning", Ohlgren makes the convincing case that

> the virtues celebrated in courtly romance – martial prowess, voluntary daring, quest for unpredictable risk, loyalty to a revered lady, solidarity of the group and largesse – have been conserved, imitated and appropriated by the urban merchant and artisan classes, who are the producers and consumers of the Robin Hood poems. The outlaw of Sherwood, then, fulfils the need for a mercantile hero to replace the knightly hero of the aristocratic romances.

Indeed, much is made of cloth in the *Gest*, as when Little John measures it out to attire Sir Richard at the Lee. This element and the business of loans are hardly the most exciting aspects of the ballad; they do point, as Ohlgren posits, to a "mercantile ideology", while chivalrous behaviour remains very much to the fore. The knight Sir Richard accordingly affords all due chivalrous respect to Robin, when he gives him sanctuary in his castle:

> You are welcome, Robin Hood,
> You are very welcome to me;
> And I thank you greatly for your comfort,

> And for your courtesy,
> And for your great kindness,
> Under the greenwood tree
> I love no man in all this world
> As much as I do thee

Similar chivalric elements also appear at the very end of the *Gest* to reinforce these associations. Here, as we have seen, not only does Robin get himself into severe financial difficulties by maintaining an expensive retinue of knights and squires ("to his great renown"), he even indulges in jocular behaviour with the king himself, daring to wallop him repeatedly in the game of pluck-buffet. Such familiar banter in the highest of all social circles demonstrates the respect that Robin now merits.

In some ways this comes across as "middle-class" wish fulfilment: an acceptance by, and admiration from, social superiors who are often considered not quite as superior as in earlier times. This makes some sense in the context of the time of the ballads. After repeated visitations by the Black Death, starting in 1348, the population of England had halved; a century later it was still recovering. The shortage of labour for once gave the initiative to the lower orders, who could demand higher wages and better working conditions. Edward III's government tried to suppress this development with the Statute of Labourers in 1351, while sumptuary laws imposed restrictions on what peasants and the "middle classes" could wear – a law against bling, in effect – to stop social climbing and people getting ideas above their station. As the general population grew in wealth, so did their resentment and disdain for such restrictive actions, just as their aspirations for change became more prominent.

From around 1450, populism became a major force in English politics, giving more people a voice of sorts. The country was in a crisis from defeat in the Hundred Years War. First came the loss of Normandy to the French in 1450, then Gascony in 1453. Soldiers, often unpaid, were returning to England and the search was undertaken for scapegoats amongst the nobility directing policy. Worst of all, the king, Henry VI, fell into periodic bouts of what is believed to be catatonic stupor, which rendered him completely incapable of running the country (his ability to do so even before this episode has been widely questioned by historians); he was not even able to recognise his newly born son and heir. One consequence of this inability was a general perception that law and order had broken down and that justice was not being served.

As political factions at court developed into armed forces, much of the country at large became disgusted at the failures of their leaders and demanded that their voice be heard. Many among them were merchants, artisans and trades people – the middling sorts at whom the Robin Hood ballads were primarily pitched. A series of rebellions broke out, the most serious being that led by Jack Cade in 1450. Richard, Duke of York, positioned himself as the leader of this discontented constituency and became a populist hero, channelling the collected power and threat of the masses to his own political ends, initially achieved in 1454 when he was elevated to the office of protector of the realm during the king's incapacity. Factional hostilities increased and the Wars of the Roses broke out the following year.

The ballads were thus popular at a time of deep political crisis and social unrest. Many of the themes in the ballads could appeal to yeomanry classes on the one hand and knightly classes on the other; as entertainment, they could appeal to all, from peasant to lord. Issues of injustice and governmental misrule might be gratifyingly righted in the cultural imagination of the Robin Hood tales, a panacea provided by the good sense of some spirited yeomen living in an idealised sylvan fastness beyond the grasp of the corrupt authorities.

Herein lies the enduring appeal of Robin Hood and why he continues to attract an audience more than half a millennium on. As a champion of justice he can be – as indeed repeatedly was – adapted as a hero by successive generations to meet the concerns of their times. Thus we see his periodic resurgence as a cultural icon through the centuries. By the mid-twentieth century he was a champion of freedom against fascist and communist authoritarianism. A current manifestation for our times is, as mentioned above, Arrow (a TV re-imagining of DC Comics' Green Arrow) who accommodates the post 9/11 and post 2008 financial crisis age. The hero, clearly based on Robin Hood, is a billionaire vigilante with a conscience (and a band of merry men and women – "Team Arrow"), who dons his hood and picks up his bow to fight against corporate corruption, terrorism and injustice to the downtrodden.

But all these literary and cultural manifestations of Robin Hood are just that – literary and cultural expressions. The various elaborations and embellishments of the tales over the last six centuries stem from the mid-fifteenth century; but, as noted at the start of this chapter, even by that stage the ballads were part of a long tradition that was already over two hundred years old. Starting with the ballads and moving forwards in time thus takes us ever further away from the real-life inspiration behind the Robin Hood legend. To draw closer to that, we must instead move backwards in time and deeper into the earlier Middle Ages.

Chapter Two - ROBIN HOOD OF SHERWOOD FOREST? THE PROBLEMS OF NAME, TIME AND PLACE

The story of Robin Hood is one based on ballads written down long after the legend had taken root. Stories evolve, adopt and change over time, so it would be rash to assume that these fifteenth-century stories faithfully reflect the first stories from at least two centuries before. Identifying a time for the launch of these stories involves some approximating though informed guesswork; but surely we are at least on solid ground with the name Robin Hood, and the places Sherwood Forest and Nottingham? Alas, no, for these may well be equally speculative.

What's in a Name?

By itself, the name Robin Hood means little. If not totally fabricated it is most likely to be an alias. This might offer us something, but medieval England provides many Robin Hoods, or variations of that name, it becomes so common as to be unhelpful. There were plenty of men called by this name, but it is also a popular catch-all name, a familiar moniker for someone of the criminal classes: the outlaw equivalent of John Doe or Joe Bloggs; or of an occupational association such as Sparks or PC Plod.

Let us start with the surname "Robinhood", which is a rarer version than the separate Christian-surname variety. There are ten recorded examples of the name between 1265 and 1322. Holt, assimilating the researches of Crook, Summerson and Palmer, follows the name to the thirteenth century, from 1261 to 1296, finding it in Sussex, London, Hampshire, Huntingdonshire, Suffolk, Essex and Berkshire, concluding that "it is plain that there is a total concentration in south-eastern England". (None of the ten names have any known association with Nottingham or Yorkshire.) He believes this to be insignificant, carefully explaining that records for the south are far more abundant than in the north, and thus far more likely to be studied. Holt concludes: "The spread can only mean that 'Robinhood' was widely known and used in counties far away from Robin's home ground of Barnsdale and Sherwood".

Holt notes the association with criminal activity among the names: Alexander Robehod, theft; Robert Robehod, sheep-rustling; John Rabunhood, murder; Gilbert Robehod, unspecified criminal charges; William Robehod, robbery. (For good measure he also throws in a thief called Little John from 1292.) All this points to Robinhood being a widely known and applied sobriquet for criminals. It should also be noted, just to confuse things, that the surname was a patronymic of other folk who were (as far as we know) completely law-abiding. Hence Katherine Robynhood, who appears on a coroner's roll from London in 1325.

However, Holt's findings, contra to his own view, may well be very significant. His conclusions are convincing if we take it as a given that Barnsdale and Sherwood were indeed Robin's stalking grounds. But as we shall see, this common assumption is one that should not be taken for granted. Holt rightly deduces that "the legend must have become a national one by the second half of the thirteenth century", and that it had spread across the south. But if we remove the assumed certainty of the more northerly location for Robin, then it might just as well be the case that the story spread from the south to the north, becoming fixed as part of the legend there only later in the Middle Ages.

The first known reference to the surname Robinhood is from Berkshire in 1261-62, William "Robehod" appearing on the memoranda roll in the exchequer. The William in question was a fugitive. In an influential article from 1984, Crook shows "there can be virtually no doubt that" that this William is the same son of a Robert le Fevre (Smith), charged elsewhere with larceny. A clerk, obviously familiar with the Robin Hood legend, altered William's surname to Robehod. Whether out of mischief, boredom, a sense of fun or because the surname served as an accurate and accepted descriptor, the clerk thereby establishes knowledge of the legend by the mid-thirteenth century. As Crook concludes:

> There is little significance in the fact that the name arises in a Berkshire context; the clerk who introduced it could have come from anywhere in England, or indeed from further afield. Whatever the geographical context in which he became aware of it, he seems to have known something of the Robin Hood legend.

Previously, the earliest known written reference to Robin Hood as a famous figure from stories and ballads was in c.1377. It is a literary one, appearing in William Langland's *Piers Plowman*, in which Sloth, a personification of one of the seven deadly sins, says: "I do not know my paternoster [Our Father] perfectly as the priest sings it / But I know rhymes of Robin Hood". Sloth also confesses his ignorance of Christ and Mary, which says something about Robin's popularity. So the alteration to the name of William Robehod in the memoranda rolls takes the legend back over a century earlier. At a stroke, this sweeps away any Robin Hood origins – either of the legend or real-life inspirations – from after the mid-thirteenth century. Characters coming after this time, such as the soldier Robert Hood of Wakefield in the early fourteenth century, a popular contender for the real Robin Hood for many, may well have contributed to the development of the legend, but they did not originate it.

The simple surname Hood was – and remains – very common. As a Christian name, Robert – for which the diminutive nickname is Robin – was also very popular in the Middle Ages, initially in France. So we can expect to see the two names be brought together on many occasions; so much so that little can be gleaned from the combination of the two in our search for the legend's origins. There are just too many possibilities. Thus historians have concentrated on Robin Hoods whose names crops up in criminal records. But again, as there were so many Robin Hood names, genuine or aliases (and it can be difficult to know always the difference) there is bound to be some representation of them in the criminal records, as for any common names (John Smith, David Jones, etc).

There are a number of criminal Robert / Robin Hoods that have attracted attention. The earliest known one enters the record at Cirencester in 1216. Robert Hood, a servant of Alexander Neckham (Nequam), a noted scholar and abbot of Cirencester Abbey, murdered Ralph of Cirencester in the abbot's garden. The exact date is not known, but must be some time from 1213 when Alexander was elected to his position. That is the sum total of our knowledge, so not very promising. There is not much to commend this figure as the inspiration for the legend; the name may be either genuine or an alias. However, as I will argue in the last chapter, it is the 1216 date that may be of more significance in this case. But Robert Hood is likely the accused's genuine name.

Other criminal Robin Hoods follow. A favourite candidate

of many historians such as Holt, Keen and Crook for the real Robin is the Robert Hod who is recorded in the Sheriff of Yorkshire's pipe roll account in 1226. Interestingly, the Sheriff at this time, Eustace of Lowdham (sometimes de Ludham), went on to become High Sheriff of Nottinghamshire and Derbyshire in 1232. Here Hod is labelled a fugitive who was in financial debt to St Peter's in York. It is widely surmised that this is the same felon who appears no less than ten times in the pipe rolls between 1225 and 1234. For the years 1228-30 the pipe rolls suggest that this is the same man who is given the nickname Hobbehod and who is recorded in abbreviated Latin as "*Rob Hood fugi*" (Robert Hood, fugitive) for 1229-30. If this is one and the same man, then we do indeed have a criminal with the right name and who lived in the "right" area – if we readily accept that this is indeed the right area. But, even if, as seems likely, it is the same character in the records, what we have on our hands is a hardened career criminal with nothing of the heroic known about him. There is no clear resolution of the hero / outlaw paradox here. And, as Knight has pointed out, "the nickname Hobbehood nowhere appears in all the Robin Hood tradition".

Another pre-1261-62 Robin Hood is "Robertus Hod de Linton" in the 1241-42 pipe rolls (there is also one William Hood recorded here). Again, that is the only information we have about him. Little wonder, then, that any criminal with the first name of Robert in the Yorkshire region comes under the scrutiny of Hood hunters. Thus we have Robert of Wetherby, sometimes linked to the Robert Hod in the previous paragraph. In 1225, the king and justiciar ordered the Sheriff of Yorkshire to "seek and take and behead Robert of Wetherby, outlaw and evildoer of our land". It seems that the Sheriff was successful because the records show that Eustace claimed two shillings "for a chain to hang Robert of Wetherby". (It has been suggested this means to hang the body on display; but at this time some men were also hung with a chain placed around their shoulders.) Then there is the xenophobic Sir Robert Thwing who, in 1231-32, headed a band that attacked foreign clergy and their properties. His *nom de guerre* was William the Avenger. But all this presupposes that the name and region of Nottingham-Sherwood-Barnsdale determine the origins of the legend. This is not necessarily the case.

Finally, there is the obvious, but usually overlooked, fact that Robert is a convenient and catchy name for any robber. As *A Song of the Times* from the reign of Henry III (1216-1272) puts it: "A *robber* is very sufficiently indicated by *Robert*" ("Competenter per *Robert*, *robbur* designatur"; italics as per the original). The writer goes on to claim: "Robert fleeces, extorts and threatens [...] Every ravenous man is the companion of Robert." The song – the surviving medium of the Robin Hood ballads, of course – reveals how names are popularly given to reflect the character of the person when he sings about those "whose crimes are sufficiently declared below, and whose names are as follows". (Note "crimes" in that passage.) Thus "by *Richard*, with much aptness, is a *rich hard* man; Gilbert is not without reason called a *guiler*; and *Geoffrey* is, if we come to the point, becomes *jo frai* [I will do it]". He explains: "Each of them has a very appropriate name, by which his own character is described [...] By these people's names, which are thus described, are denoted the habit, and fraud, and works of many men."

As already mentioned, Robin is a nickname for Robert. Robert Hood as Robber Hood? The above paragraphs, especially the one directly above, offer strong and very contemporary evidence for this. Even in the twenty-first century, thieves, muggers and criminals are known for wearing hoods: as effective a way of shielding one's features now as in the Middle Ages.

In sum, the name Robin Hood tells us very little other than it was an appellation popularly associated with criminals. It is highly unlikely that there was an original figure genuinely called Robin Hood who lies behind the legend; it is therefore almost certainly futile to search for him by his name. If the legend of Robin Hood is based on a real person, it is far more probable that the name Robin Hood evolved to become the literary and cultural tag for someone with an entirely different name.

Is Timing Everything?

In discussing Robin Hood's name we have already considered important aspects of the timing of the Robin Hood legend. Other clues and even outright statements in the ballads indicate a range of times in which to look for the setting of the original stories. Once again, these lead to much speculative assertions, often based on an over-optimistic credence in dubious sources.

We have discussed the immediate context of the troubled environment in mid-fifteenth century England at the time of the surviving Robin Hood ballads: political tensions, the beginnings of Wars of the Roses and a perception of break down in law and order. Thus Robin's name comes up in voices of discontent beyond the ballads. In 1441 in Norfolk, we encounter a gang of yeomen and labourers who set themselves up on a road to attack travellers, vowing to kill a local member of the gentry. Their chant was: "We are Robynhodesmen – war, war, war!" This military perception of the Robin Hood character is significant, as will be discussed in chapters four and five. As Maddern, in her study of violence in East Anglia 1422-42, notes of this episode, it offers an example of men justifying righteous violence in their perceived just cause, enabling

the individual to identify good violence from bad. Robin Hood's exploits in the outlaw bands, for instance [...] could appear moral in fifteenth-century terms. He punished the wicked, was a manly and successful fighter, and claimed to be a supporter of the king's law. No wonder, then, that the name of Robin Hood might be used by the violent in justifying their actions.

During the uprisings of 1450, the greatest of which was Jack Cade's rebellion, rebel captains in the south appointed themselves such names as "Robin Hood" and, less intimidating to modern ears, "King of the Fairies". Harvey, in his monograph on 1450, notes that this was "a trick used by poachers". In 1469 in Northumberland, Sir John Conyers called himself Robin Mend-all when he joined Warwick's rebellion against Edward IV. In 1498 Roger Marshal caused a significant disturbance of the peace under the name of Robin Hood when he was charged with threatening the men of Walsall. However, this may have simply been a case of boisterous, laddish behaviour that got of hand which resulted in a beating and then developed into riotous assembly; it may also have had some connection with the lively May Games celebrations.

All this shows that by the fifteenth century the Robin Hood legend was not merely widely known in culture but that the hero was also replicated in popular action – a case of life imitating art. This points to a tradition of the appropriation of Robin Hood's name. The taking-on of Robin's name – rather than it be ascribed to others by record-keepers and writers – was already likely established in the fourteenth century, as we shall discover in the next section on place, where we will look at the Hoods of Wakefield.

In which period of history did those closest in time to the legend place Robin? Late medieval Scottish chronicles lead the way. This shows that the folklore had reached as far north as it had south. Having encountered various Robins in ballads, plays and criminal records, we now come to meet him in chronicle form, delineated as a real historical figure.

As noted in chapter one, Andrew Wyntoun's *Original Chronicle* from circa 1420 mentions both Robin and Little John. For the years 1283-85 he writes:

Little John and Robin Hood
Outlaws who were acclaimed good,
In Inglewood and Barnsdale
They in this time did their travail [ie, work, endeavours]

Note that Little John comes first in this pairing. Wyntoun, an Augustinian prior of St Sers Inch, wrote this when an old man, which connects him to a much earlier period. Bradbury has noted another Hood in the chronicle for the year 1342, leading a daring raid on Roxburgh in which he and his men escalade the castle and overcome its garrison, before departing with much plunder. Whether these are two different Hoods or a confusion over one is impossible to say. Medieval chronicles are often troubled by inconsistencies and inaccuracies.

Robin and Little John reappear in Walter Bower's *Scotichronicon* from the 1440s. Like his fellow Scot Wyntoun, Bower was an Augustinian canon at St Andrews. Bower, although probably familiar with his predecessor's work, must also have been influenced by his continuation of John of Fordun's *Scotichronicon*, written in the second half of the fourteenth century, to which, in true medieval chronicle tradition, Bower amended and added as he thought fit, without notifying the reader where he had done this. It is now believed that Bower's Robin Hood comments are his own. He places Robin Hood earlier than Wyntoun under the year 1266, where he writes:

> There then arose from the disinherited and outlaws that famous cut-throat Robin Hood, with Little John and their accomplices, of whom the foolish people are so exceedingly fond of celebrating in both tragedy and comedy, and their delight in hearing jesters and bards sing of them in other romances.

Bower goes on to tell a tale of Robin, "an outlaw among the woodland briars and thorns", listening devoutly to mass when he is attacked by a viscount and his men; Robin and his men beat off the assault and pocket some nice plunder in the process.

The date of 1266 and the reference to the disinherited (*exheredatis*) are important here: they give the context for Robin Hood as the aftermath of the 1264-65 baronial revolt in England in which supporters of the losing side, led by Simon de Montfort, faced punishment by the loss of their family lands. According to Bower, Robin and Little John form part of this group, continuing the struggle after the death of Montfort at the battle of Evesham in 1265. Bower thus provides a significant connection to the rebel Roger Godberd, one of the strongest contenders for the development of the Robin Hood legends. (He is discussed in the final chapter.)

A third Scottish chronicler has been the most influential on the timing of the legend, especially for cultural representations of Robin Hood. John Major (Maior), born in 1467, had his *History of Greater Britain* published in 1521. In this he writes of Robin Hood and Little John being active during the reign of

Richard the Lionheart (1189-99): "at the time of King Richard, according to my estimate". From this we have Robin as the hero of numerous recent cinema movies set in the 1190s, resisting corrupt rule, especially during the absence of King Richard, who is captured by enemies on his way back from the crusades. In his stead, the avaricious Prince John is plotting a coup, bleeding the country dry of money and denying true justice.

This timing was widely accepted as early as the end of the sixteenth century and became popularised by the Robin Hood / "Earl of Huntingdon" plays of Anthony Munday. (The Elizabethan era saw a flourishing of renewed interest in all things chivalric.) By the nineteenth century, the period was still strongly favoured in the hugely successful novel, *Ivanhoe*, by Sir Walter Scott. Not only did this novel receive a massive readership since its publication at the end of 1819 but, in an echo of early transmissions of the legend, it was also a box-office hit in its dramatised form: at one point in London, five theatres were simultaneously putting on productions of *Ivanhoe*. TV series and films of the original novel have kept audiences connecting this period to the Robin Hood legend, as have the numerous Hollywood films and TV series with Robin as their main subject. They are helped in this by the fact that John, whether as king or plotting prince, can hardly be bettered as an evil character, needing little embellishment to render him so. (Some revisionist historians have tried to portray John in a more positive light, but without conviction; he really was quite a piece of work, or, as Vincent judges him, "a rotter".)

John Major also contributed to another part of the Robin Hood image: that of the charity conscious robber.

There flourished those most famous robbers, Robert Hood,

an Englishman, and Little John, who lay waiting in the woods, but only stole the goods of the wealthy. They took no one's life, unless he either assaulted them or resisted them defending his property. Through this plundering, Robert supported 100 bowmen, ready fighters every one [...] The deeds of this Robert are sung all over England. He would allow no woman to suffer injustice, nor would he steal from the poor, but rather he enriched them from the plunder seized from the abbots. I condemn the robberies of this man, but of all of the robbers he was the most human.

Here is presented a Robin clearly identifiable to modern audiences. But it resounds too strongly of the ballads' version, presented as fact.

As for this dating of the Robin legend, despite how influential it continues to be, there is absolutely nothing to support it other than Major's assertion. That the further each successive chronicler is in time from the origins of the legend, the further back in time he places it – by nearly a century in all – goes to show how elastic, and almost meaningless, these datings are. All that said, we are in highly speculative territory; we must remember that absence of evidence is not evidence of absence. The Robin Hood legend may indeed have started in the 1190s, but this is unlikely; it may also have started earlier (more improbably) or later. We do not know.

It is worth remembering that medieval chroniclers could also write of mythical figures as historical ones, such as Prester John. And as Pollard observes: "No fifteenth-century English chronicler made an attempt to place the outlaws in 'real time'. For these fifteenth century commentators, Robin and Little John are nothing more than the central characters of vulgar tales, or lewd ribaldries."

There is little profit in looking for time clues in the earliest surviving ballads. Much has been made of social, monetary and cultural indicators in these, but, overall, they mix and match characteristics of the age that the audience was living in with earlier ones. Just as cultural icons such as Sherlock Holmes have been transplanted into the twenty-first century for modern viewers to keep the story relevant, so it is – and ever was – with Robin. This was especially the case given the oral tradition of the tales before printed versions. The ballads do have some anachronistic inconsistencies in this regard (they are assembled, after all); the role of the Sheriff is one. But such anachronisms persist to this day in retelling the story, the *Robin Hood* film of 2018 taking all sorts of liberties with the medieval world to make it more attractive (as they perceive it) to the modern one.

One fact in the *Gest* much trawled over is the reference to the king, Edward. But again this tells us little. As mentioned, this could be one of at least three, and possibly, four Edwards. Three definite possibilities are Edward I (1272-1307), Edward II (1307-27) and Edward III (1327-77), the last being favoured by some, the first by others. Holt believes that the *Gest* may have been written as early as circa 1450 but, as Ohlgren argues, the composition or compilation could range from Henry V's reign (1413-22) to the end of his successor's, Henry VI (1461). This opens up the possibility of Edward IV, who came to the throne in March 1461.

The *Gest* reveals little of King Edward in its pages: he is "our handsome king"; Robin attests to his strength when Edward strikes him down with a blow; he likes to indulge in a bit of knock-about macho banter; and he is "very tall". This does not get us far. Edward I and Edward IV were renowned for their heights, both being over six foot tall: Edward I has the nickname Longshanks, while Edward IV's skeleton measures in at nearly six foot four inches, and he was considered a very good looking man. Even the non-martial Edward II, not a likely contender as someone who went in for the rough and tumble of male play-fighting (not of the sort depicted in the *Gest*, anyway), was an imposing figure, one contemporary chronicler describing him as "fair of body and great of strength". (But as Gillingham tellingly adds: "sadly he was also little of brain.")

If the ballads are really set during the reign of Edward III, then the tales are already historical fiction, and could alter at the whim of writers composing at different times. Pollard observes of the *Gest*:

> One would be surprised if listeners or readers thought it other than a fiction. One would similarly be amazed if late-fifteenth-century readers of Malory's *Morte d'Arthur* took literally as historical facts the stories he told of the knights of the round table.

There is much to be said for this judgment; but fiction and legend have a way of morphing themselves into accepted "facts", or half-facts in popular perceptions over time.

Location, Location, Location

So far, so much speculation. But the one given we can surely rely on is that the Robin Hood legend originates in the northern midlands and South Yorkshire. Whether Barnsdale, Nottingham or Sherwood should take pride of place is hotly debated, but the consensus overwhelming acknowledges that these places constitute Robin Hood country. (Given the massive pull of the tourist industry, "ownership" of Robin can be fiercely contested, as witnessed over the original naming of Doncaster Airport as Robin Hood Airport.) But should this consensus be so readily accepted? No.

Much energy and ingenuity has been devoted to identifying the exact locations of Robin's activities in his established territory. There is no disputing a greenwood hideaway for Robin and his men: where else but in a forest would a band of outlaws wish to hide? Medieval chroniclers repeatedly refer to *silvatici*, those that live in forests, denoting outlaws and rebels. And to waylay travellers making their way through forests, stretches of the Great North Road and its medieval branch of Watling Street (named in the *Gest*) make perfect sense for this area. Sherwood Forest was already notorious for banditry in the twelfth century. Three cantos into the *Gest* we are told "Robin stood in Barnsdale / And leant against a tree". The Yorkshire Barnsdale is even further into the more unruly medieval north. (There was also a large medieval wood, as opposed to forest, in Barnsdale, Rutland, nearly eighty miles to the south-east, just to confuse issues.) The setting works. But then again so would any major road through isolated wooded and forested areas.

Historians have therefore understandably sought Robin Hoods along this geographical line and proximate area. We have already met Robin Hood of Wakefield. Records show that Wakefield, only some twelve miles from Barnsdale, had a long history of an actual Hood family in the Middle Ages, dating back to at least the early 1200s. Holt believes that this offers "the most realistic and detailed of all the locations of the legend" and the connection to the legend "is unlikely to be accidental". The first suggestion can be contested; the second can be neatly explained in Holt's own words, which offers a realistic explanation: "Either the Hoods of Wakefield gave Robin to the world, or they absorbed the tale of the outlaw into family traditions or their neighbours and descendants came to associate the two. Of these the last is the most likely". And it is a common surname. There will be plenty of other Hoods out there around the country with a similar genealogy, but these are ignored because they are not in "official" Robin Hood country.

There are two major problems with the Nottingham-Sherwood-Barnsdale dominance of the Robin Hood legend. The first is the question of the area involved. Sherwood Forest was much larger in the Middle Ages – Barraclough's estimates in 2018 give the thirteenth-century forest the size of about 100,000 acres ("a fifth of the county") – so it was the most suitable place for concealment in the region. Even so, as other historians have pointed out, the whole area covering Robin's activities as set out in the ballads could be travelled across north to south in a day. This is an unfeasibly compact area for an outlaw gang. This bears no comparison to the reality of the movements of another, nineteenth-century outlaw on horseback, also considered to be a latter day Robin Hood: Jesse James. He travelled across vast distances to not only find new stalking grounds, but primarily to avoid the law. There is no practical sense to Robin carving a prosperous living by haunting the same ambush sites year in and year out; it would be too obvious and too dangerous, greatly increasing the chances of capture.

Furthermore, how would Robin hide his large company of 140 men in so small an area? In one of the ballads, he is even depicted as living in a house, indicating a fixed position. How dull-witted or completely starved of resources must the Sheriff have been to have failed to have tracked down this famous robber and his small army on his doorstep? (Clearly he was not short of resources at all, as Robin was able to make a healthy living by repeatedly plundering them.) The ballads all appear to take place in sunny, leafy spring or summer; what happened in winter when the trees were bare of their cover, and thus so were the outlaws? And what of the tell-tale smoke from all those fires needed to cook all that venison?

But this should also lead us to address another, even bigger problem: why should we trust the ballads as hard evidence? Why, apart from their chance survival, should we accept their scene setting as "official" Robin Hood territory? The ballads were written, and the plays performed, primarily for entertainment, not education. Yet historians have overwhelmingly concentrated their research on looking for Robin Hoods in this hallowed area, as if hopefully vindicating the historical accuracy and dependability of these ballads.

The whole Sherwood focus is based on mid-fifteenth century ballad survivals composed over two hundred years after the likely origins of the legend. We have seen that the story was known as far north as Scotland and across the whole south of England. In the south, we know of thirteenth-century scribes who have written the name Robin Hood into its court records, we have a Robert Hood murderer in Cirencester, and also in the south we have an exclusive dominance of the Robinhood surname. What if there were ballad traditions in areas other than official Robin Hood country, in which the Robin Hood tales were played out in their localities? These may have been written down and lost; they may simply have died out with the impermanence of oral tradition; or, over the two centuries and more, Nottingham and Sherwood endured and won out against regional competitors?

These are important considerations given the main transmission of the legend through ballads and performances. There was no copyright version of the legend; it could – and almost certainly was – adapted for different audiences. Think of comedians on tour. When they are performing in a new town, more times than not they will joke about local aspects of that town or city, tailoring their material to the home audience. Listeners to Radio 4's *Sorry I Haven't a Clue* will be familiar with the comedic ritual at the start of each programme when the host town is jovially disparaged. Rock and pop bands tell the audience they are playing to that night that they love them and that they are the best; and then say exactly the same thing the next night in another part of the country, or in a different country altogether. Such expressions win over audiences through flattery and humour.

The best comparison of all is with that seasonal favourite, the pantomime. The actors play fast and loose with the original scripts, often adlibbing freely, and invariably pleasing the audience with local references. The pantomime found its origins in the *commedia dell'arte*, popular in sixteenth-century Europe, and these origins can in turn be traced further back into Roman times. Another name for these is *commedia improvviso*, as the companies performing them adapted a cast of stock characters (readily provided by Robin Hood, his Merry Men, the Sheriff) and improvised with them and their place of performance. The Robin Hood tales fit readily into this performance context. The focus has been entirely on Sherwood Forest and its environs because that is all we have. But it might not be enough.

Chapter Three - OUTLAWS AND PUNISHMENT IN MEDIEVAL ENGLAND

Punishment

If Robin Hood really did die as portrayed in the ballads, he got off more lightly than many of his fellow felons who faced the full rigours of the justice system. In "Robin and Guy of Gisborne" and "Robin Hood and the Monk", both Little John and Robin are extremely fortunate to be freed from prison by their outlaw band. Their fate otherwise would have been to end up on a gibbet.

Punishment was usually monetary, physical or fatal. Prisons were few and far between; their primary purpose was to hold those being charged until a court could clear them or impose a swift punishment on them. (There were exceptions, not least among the higher ranks of society, when imprisonment could be lengthy.) Harsh sentencing was not simply the response of the authorities to a fear of a break down in law and order and a possible uprising by the common folk, as happened most notably in 1381 and 1450, but it responded also to the demands for justice made by these very same common folk. Thus in 1389, public opinion led to the successful petitioning of parliament to limit pardons for violent crimes. It was not the case that the authorities had been feeling lenient; instead, these pardons were often granted in exchange for the prisoner signing up with the army. Government commissioners would trawl prisons to boost recruitment, as in 1284 in readiness for Edward I's Gascony campaign.

Public executions were deliberate visual displays intended as deterrents, but even court cases could be spectacles of theatre, as with trials of ordeal: trial by water, iron, and battle. Trial by iron involved carrying a burning hot brand over a specific distance. The hand was then bound. After three days, the bandaging was removed; an infected hand indicated guilt. Trial by water, well known as a test for witches, took precedence as the Middle Ages progressed. The accused was put into blessed water: the purified water would, it was believed, reject the guilty (who floated) and accept the innocent (who sank – hopefully not for too long). After these trials acquittal or punishment was prompt: in the 1170s one Ailward failed trial by water and was immediately blinded and castrated. The acquittal rate for water was around sixty per cent.

Trial by battle would have been the best option for Robin, Little John and their men had they faced trial following their imprisonments, especially as the usual instrument of "battle" was the wooden staff, so common in the tales of Robin Hood. Obviously, God would favour the side of the righteous with victory. The courts did not want a fatality in the combat; if the guilty party were to die, the proper authorities would see to it.

The "battle" was, in effect, a bludgeoning match. A legal treatise from the thirteenth century advised that a good set of incisors was advantageous for success. An account from 1456 – and thus directly contemporaneous with the Robin Hood ballads – offers a dramatic depiction of trial by battle. After a cudgel had broken:

> For a long time they fought together with their fists, rested themselves, resumed fighting, rested once more; and then went head to head. They both bit with their teeth so that the leather of their clothes and their flesh was torn all over their bodies. And then the false appealer threw the meek innocent opponent to the ground and bit him in the testicles, causing

the innocent man to cry out [...] The innocent recovered to his knees, in turn bit the false appealer on the nose and jabbed his thumb in his eye, causing the appealer to cry out and beg for mercy.

Apparently a bite on the balls can be quite motivating. The defeated man was granted a last confession and then hanged.

Violence – and fear of it – was a dominating feature of everyday society. Violent crime in England at the end of the Middle Ages ran at ten times that of the nineteenth-century. In a world of manual labour, dangerous tools lay all around: mattocks, shovels, axes, hammers, knives (in one of the ballads, Robin uses an "Irish" knife to disfigure Gisborne's face). A trial from 1434 examined the death of Richard Tarcel, killed by Elesius Tomesson who had been wielding a hedge stake. Swords were not used just for running people through and hacking them as in the ballads; in a psychological twisted case from Lincolnshire in the early fourteenth century, one Ralph Tokel uses his sword to cut off the soles from his victim's feet. The permanent threat of war meant the nation had to be prepared for violence: the 1285 Statute of Winchester ordered every male between sixteen and sixty to undergo martial training and to maintain arms, stipulating the bow and arrows. But the statute's main preoccupation is with crime, as it makes clear from its opening: "Forasmuch as from day to day, robberies, murder and arsons be more often used than they have been heretofore..."

Law and order is a constant preoccupation of society in any age, but at the time of the ballads it was a particularly high concern. A king's most important roles were those of *miles*, *iudex* and *sacerdos* – knight (ie, warrior), judge and priest. Henry VI certainly fulfilled the last role well (one historian called him "a pious muff") but failed at the first two: around

1455 the northern chronicler John Hardyng wrote

> In every shire with jacks and helmets clean
> Misrule does rise, and makes neighbours war.
> The weaker goes beneath, as is often seen,
> The mightiest his quarrel with prefer
> That poor men's causes are set back too far

He goes on to lament that there is no peace but instead killing and rioting because there is no justice. A violent environment like this calls out for a righteous hero and defender of the weak, if the king is not able to protect his subjects and punish the guilty.

The ultimate fate for captured criminals was a shameful death on the gibbet. Some eighty per cent of criminal executions were for property crime. Hanging was the form of execution most feared by those of a knightly and noble status, as it associated them with the lowly criminal classes. A case from northern France in the late fourteenth-century tells of a noble condemned to be hung; his relations, to avoid the shame on the family of a public hanging, arranged for the guilty man's "escape" so that they could strangle him instead. Hanging would have been the execution for any real "Robin Hood" who was caught for thieving. (There were regional variations of capital punishment: on the south coast options included being flung from the cliffs of Dover, buried alive or shackled to a rock just off the coast waiting for the tide to come in.)

Excessive use of the death penalty sometimes led to a reaction against it in later medieval England, which might chime with audiences of William of Cloudesley (see below) and Robin Hood when the heroes escape the gibbet. When, in 1285, rape was made a capital felony, juries routinely found in favour of the defendant. A fourteen-year-old thief in Westmoreland in 1292 should have been hung for his crimes, but the judges shaved two years off his age so as a juvenile he would escape execution. Locals refused to assist in the hanging of a pregnant woman condemned to execution in 1258; her pregnancy should have ensured a stay of execution until after delivery of the baby. The great mortality from plague and war from the mid-fourteenth century may well have put a higher price on life.

A sense of proportionate justice was important to the general population. There are reported cases of convicted felons on the gallows being rescued at the last minute. But two hangmen who helped one to escape in 1293 were themselves hung. Crowds might also shout for mercy for the condemned; authorities, fearing public disorder, occasionally acceded to these wishes for clemency. But the quality of mercy could be very strained. In 1221, Thomas of Eldersfield lost a trial by combat but instead of being hung he was shown mercy: he was blinded and castrated. Bartlett recounts that "the eyes were thrown to the ground, the testicles used as footballs, the local lads kicking them playfully at the girls". As flirtation, it is not quite what might be found in an Arthurian romance, but it does remind us that spectacularly violent punishment could prove popular.

There was even a patron saint of condemned men: St Thomas Cantilupe. Even before his canonisation, Thomas was invoked as a quite literally last minute measure by men on the gallows – and even after they had been hung. In 1285 the thief Walter Eghe was cut down after hanging, but recovered and was granted a royal pardon; his survival was deemed a divine sign of his innocence. (He fared better than an Oxfordshire man who, unbeknownst to the ineffectual hangman, survived the gibbet only to be buried alive.) When the notorious murderer William Cragh was about to be hung on a gibbet in Swansea in 1291, a lady prayed to St Thomas. When the ladder was kicked away Cragh suffered the agonies of execution, as noted by an observer: his face was black and swollen, his eyes protruding, his neck, throat, nose and mouth were bloody, and his tongue was livid and thick, having been cut by his teeth and "hung out of his mouth as long as a man's finger". But by the next day he was up and about and went on to live for another eighteen years at least.

In France in 1396 William the Breton must have been feeling exceptionally fortunate at his hanging which took place in Le Mans. Each time the hanging was attempted, the halter broke and William dropped to the ground. Even when his leg broke he was forced to struggle back up to the gibbet. But repeated failures suggested that celestial aid was at hand. William, in pain but greatly relieved, was reprieved from execution and put in a carriage to take him back to prison. Here his luck failed him: on the return to gaol the carriage overturned in an accident and William was crushed to death. As far-fetched as tales of medieval outlaws can be, sometimes they were outdone by reality.

Another possible reason for the apparent popularity of anti-monastic sentiment in the Robin Hood ballads is the harshness of abbey courts. In the late twelfth century, the abbot of Glastonbury condemned Ralph le Taburer to hanging; after burial he was exhumed and his corpse hung from a tree. In the late thirteenth century the abbot of Evesham's court executed a thief over 4d, causing outrage and a government response against such extreme sanctions: a statue of 1278/9 made 12d the measure of a man's life. Locals had their revenge against the abbey of Bury St Edmunds during the great revolt of 1381: the prior of the abbey, John of Cambridge, had his head cut off and mounted on a pole; this was then used in a macabre puppet performance with the decapitated head of the chief justice of England. As a contemporary source reports: "Playing with their heads they put the head of the prior to the head of the justice, now to the ear as if giving advice, now to his mouth as if showing friendship [ie, kissing]." The beheading of the monk and his page Little John and Much do not seem quite so shocking against this real-life context.

Crime and Criminals in Late Medieval England

One of the ironies of Robin Hood as a champion of justice is that his own "actions" contributed to this overall sense of disorder. He and his Merry Men were poachers. For all Robin's loyalty to the king, he drastically thins his deer herds, shooting them and seizing game in the king's forests. For most of the population, but not those employed by the crown as foresters and warreners, poaching might be considered a victimless crime: the king could afford the losses; people needed to eat and there was plenty of game to go round. England's extensive royal forests were a permanent and massive reminder of the division between rulers and ruled. The forests had their own laws; indeed, in 1217 these were hived off from Magna Carta for their own charter. (This is why we have the term Magna Carta: previously, it was known as the Articles of the Barons; with the separating out of the few forest clauses what was left was the "Big Charter" – Magna Carta.) The strength of feeling about entitlement to game is in some ways indicated by an event in Sherwood Forest from 1276. Two archers were arrested for poaching and detained by the steward of Sherwood. A gang some twenty strong arrived with bows and swords, beat up the guards, smashed in the windows of the steward's house and freed the poachers. Perhaps one appeal of the Robin Hood stories is that though not factual, they were based on identifiable or believable events.

In the fifteenth century persecutions in the forest courts for poaching game were rare. In Buckinghamshire in 1438-39, Philip Pagham was pardoned for poaching venison in the royal forest of Bernwood. Shortly after Henry VII came to the throne in 1485, he ordered a crackdown by re-enacting the 1390 Game Law. He probably needed to, given that just one man, William of Holcombe of Lymington, killed eighteen deer between June 1484 and January 1488. Pollard's study of this area reveals that "poachers ranged from the knightly through yeoman, butchers, bakers, bucketmakers and vagabonds". He notes that most poaching was undertaken by sole individuals, or at most in gangs of five, taking one animal at a time: "The most serious was a gang of six (a yeoman, a husbandman and labourers) who broke into a park to take game." That Robin's retinue amounted to 140 men would indicate poaching on an industrial scale if that had been his only enterprise.

Robbery and, of course murder, were far more serious – and more profitable. There are six of the former crimes and a dozen of the latter in the first ballads. Medieval England offers a positive cornucopia of examples to demonstrate the extent of both of these crimes. A look at a few actual crimes, criminals and their gangs will reveal similarities (and dissimilarities) with the Robin Hood legends, but also show how reality could easily prove a valuable source for fiction. We will focus here on the later Middle Ages which have a greater contemporary resonance for the ballads.

In 1317 two cardinals and the bishop elect of Durham, Lewis (Louis) de Beaumont, were seized by Gilbert Middleton. The attack took place on the road heading north between Darlington and Durham. A local contemporary source notes: "Gilbert de Middleton met them with a large force of armed men […] They neither kidnapped the cardinals nor the others, but robbed them all instead". The bishop elect, however, was held until he "was released from imprisonment once a sum of money and hostages had been handed over". A national chronicle, however, does not mention the bishop at all but notes with satisfaction later that "Gilbert was taken to London [...] There he was drawn, hanged and disembowelled and his head cut off". The robbery received attention abroad, provoking the rage of Pope Boniface VIII.

This has obvious features familiar to Robin Hood's legend: ambushing; taking money and then letting men go; ransoming; and the targeting of high-ranking church officials. Lewis may well have been an unworthy cleric: he had come in for criticisms that he was unsuitable to be bishop, with rumours spreading that he did not even know Latin.

Not uncommon, especially for the north, was for traveling parties to hire bodyguards, as the Durham group did. Often these bodyguards were in fact local bandits (*schavaldores*), so they operated a form of protection racket at the same time as their banditry. At one point Durham was spending a massive twenty per cent of its annual income on such protection. This sort of enterprise is more likely to have supported 140 men than mere poaching.

There are various political and military layers to this incident, not least with a context of Scottish wars and raids. The military aspect is important: war saw a proliferation of large armed bands in a time when justice took secondary place to military imperatives. As I argue in the next chapters, a background of war offers more potential for the origins of the Robin Hood legend than even justice. Prestwich has noted numerous significant criminals operating in this region around the time of this incident, including Jack the Irishman, "notorious for his exploits in the north, such as the rape and abduction of Lady Clifford".

Two criminal gangs that acquired national notoriety were those of the Folvilles of Leicestershire and the Coterels of Derbyshire. The chronicler Henry Knighton tales of how in 1331 the Folvilles and Coterels kidnapped Sir Richard Willoughby, a royal justice, and held him to ransom. If proof were needed to show what a rum bunch this lot were, the chronicler calls their leader Richard Folville, "wild and bold and prone to violence". Richard was the less than respectable rector of the church of Teigh (in Rutland – where, as noted previously, there is another Barnsdale). Court records from 1332 point to Eustace Folville as "chief of their organisation". These records provide an exhausting litany of their wrongdoings: stealing four horses; theft of a cask of wine; hostage taking; robbery of two horses and harnesses; stealing three oxen, a bull, capons and hens; driving off 29 sheep; seizing of a mare and colts; stealing from a church; and various substantial money thefts.

The records describe the gang as "common thieves, robbers and slayers of men" – a stock legal phrase but one that the Folvilles and Coterels did their best to live up to. Both gangs were, despite – indeed, because of – their reputations, hired for nefarious practices by churchmen: the Coterels to attack a "rival" vicar, the Folvilles to destroy a water mill belonging to a competitor. Richard Folville was arrested after a struggle in which an officer of the law was killed; the errant pastor was pulled out of his church and beheaded. The fame of these criminals was such that the Folvilles join Robin Hood in the pages of one version of Langland's *Piers Plowman* which refers to "false men with their Folville's laws" (these "laws" being the misrule and anarchy of banditry). For some historians, the Folvilles offer potential for the Robin Hood origins. But their brutality against all, and not just the Church; their lack of any heroic attributes; and, most of all the time they lived in: all mitigate against this possibility. But popular distortions of their actions may well have fed into later versions.

The Mynors gang terrorised the Wolverhampton area in the early fifteenth century. An indictment of 1411-12 tells of five of them who "with force and arms came to the church of Wolverhampton and in the same church without reason maliciously assaulted Richard, parson of Wolverhampton, and mutilated and injured him". The local community was so outraged they dispensed some vigilante justice: they "fell on them and mutilated and killed" them all. But other members of the gang – "notorious thieves and robbers, ambushers of highways and despoilers of fields" – were still active later in the year, committing murder. The following year they engage in local economic warfare, destroying water mills and going on a plundering spree. Apart from the large gang and violence to a churchman (though not a monk), there is little of the Robin Hood figure here: the destruction of crops in fields and mills needed for the making of basic food hit at ordinary people, not just the undeserving rich. But local politics were often intricate and divisive. Both the Mynors and the Folvilles received local help; whether this was provided through fear, admiration, connections or a combination of these is impossible to determine.

Our last case brings in one of the Merry Men. In the early fifteenth century the criminous clerk Robert Stafford, mentioned previously, identified himself as Friar Tuck during his depredations and poaching across Sussex. In a commission of 1417, this chaplain of Lindfield is accused of being an "evildoer" who has "entered with force and arms, warrens and chases [...] and carried off deer, hares, rabbits, pheasants and partridges and burned the houses and lodges" of the keepers, who he "threatened with death or bodily mutilation". The commission refers to him as "Frere Tuk" three times. The scribe was not familiar with the name, calling it "unusual". This may mean a number of things, including either that Friar Tuck was not yet well-known, either as an individual or as an associate of Robin Hood, or that the scribe, unlike Stafford, had simply not heard of these tales.

For some historians Stafford understandably makes a convenient Friar Tuck. This might makes sense by name alone (there may have been earlier references) but the phenomenon of churchmen as criminals was nothing new. In 1370, Archdeacon William Beverley was accused of malicious homicide. The Folville gang boasted at least three men of the cloth within their ranks. And the famous Henry II versus Thomas Becket dispute in the twelfth century was caused in large part by clergy benefiting from canon (church) law to avoid being prosecuted in secular courts (harsher than church ones) for crimes they had committed.

Crime Fiction and Fact

Popular culture in the Middle Ages saw a two-way movement between real-life criminals and fictional ones. As Storer recently observed: "There is no denying that contemporaries were quick to link the deeds of fictitious outlaws with the criminals of their age." We have seen this in the addition of the name Robin Hood to various official documents; we have also seen movement the other way with the Folvilles being incorporated into a version of *Piers Plowman*. Just as today the crime genre is hugely popular (be it in film, on TV, in literature; and be it fictional or factual), so it was in the Middle Ages. Robin Hood was just one of a number of famous tales.

The story of *Adam Bell, Clim of the Clough and William of Cloudesley* are deserving of attention here (more tales, closer to the Robin Hood origins, are considered in the following chapter). The popularity of Adam and his comrades was widespread in late medieval England and in numerous printed editions beyond the sixteenth century and even "until the nineteenth", says Phillips. It was the second outlaw tale to appear in print form (after Robin Hood). In 1432 parliamentary records for Wiltshire reveal a clerks' list of fictitious outlaws: Adam, Clim and William are included alongside Robin Hood, Little John, Much the Millers Son, Reynold Greenleaf and Will Scarlett – esteemed company, indeed.

The Robin Hood parallels are present from the start, with the *Adam Bell* story opening, as Hahn puts it, "in the merry greenwood, where men roam freely and enjoy untroubled relations with nature and each other". The original tale invites the audience, as in the Robin Hood ballads, "to attend and listen, gentlemen". It is set in the north-west (the wildest of all England's areas) in Carlisle and the nearby forest of Inglewood, where men with bows and arrows hunt for deer. William is the finest archer among the three outlaw poachers and the only wedded one. He wishes to go to Carlisle to be with his wife, Alice, and their children. He ignores advice not to venture into town. When there, he demands food and drink from his wife, and possibly other favours (that "she pleased him […] with what she had" might suggest this was a conjugal visit). Betrayed by an old woman, the citizenry of Carlisle attack his house. He, armed with bow, sword and buckler, is supported by Alice with a poleaxe, no less (obviously she was a lady of some physical strength; few households would have a poleaxe lying around). The Sheriff burns them out of the house and William, after a spirited resistance, is thrown into "a fortified dungeon". The Sheriff promises to hang him soon.

When Adam and Clim hear of this they mount a rescue mission. They trick their way into the walled town, breaking the porter's neck as they do so and take his keys. They shoot the Justice and the Sheriff with their bows, free William from his restraints, and, with super-hero strength, skill and endurance, fend off the whole town (slaughtering half of it, it would seem) before escaping back to the woods. Here William is reunited with his family.

"These rugged men" (also called "yeomen" in the tale) then head off to London with William's eldest son to seek the king's pardon (rather optimistically or dim-wittedly one would have thought after the carnage at Carlisle, where they had "slain three hundred men and more"). Eschewing the niceties of preliminary polite etiquette, they burst in on the king and then kneel before him. The king calls them "thieves" (not killers, though), and orders them to be bound and hanged. The queen, in a customary medieval role of espousing mercy, pleads successfully to the king to show clemency.

The tale ends (no spoiler alert needed by now) with an archery contest. This culminates with William tying his seven-year-old son to a stake and boasting that from 120 paces distant he can split an apple placed on his head. If he fails, all three men will be hanged. (The possible consequences for the poor boy are not raised, be they fatal, physical maiming or sheer mental trauma). William does his proto-William Tell act and he and Adam and Clim are rewarded with money and royal posts, and Alice is to be brought to court as the queen's "chief gentlewoman". The three men sally off to Rome so that the Pope can obligingly absolve them of their sins before they return to the king's service in which "all three died as good men. Thus ends the lives of these good yeomen: God send them eternal bliss. And may all those who shoot with bows never miss heaven!"

The influence of the outlaw Robin Hood is clear throughout: great bravery and martial feats; poaching; extensive violence; superb archery skills; loyalty of comrades; trickery and disguise; ultimate deference and loyalty to the king; joining the king's service. Andrew Wyntoun, in his *Original Chronicle* of circa 1420, claims that a real-life Robin Hood operated in both Barnsdale and Inglewood. And, as noted above, William's story was known in Wiltshire in the south by 1432 when the names of the heroes of Robin and his men were added to an official document.

Thus the links between fictional outlaws and actual criminals was frequently and deliberately blurred. Hahn's extremely perceptive comments on *Adam Bell* apply equally to Robin Hood and Sherwood, Nottingham and Barnsdale:

The resorts to specifics (on weapons and legal matters) and to local realism – in particular, the allusions to Inglewood Forest and Carlisle in the north, and the recourse to the king's court in the capital – sets the action in a 'medievalesque' framework [...] This deployment of 'faux history' to ground extravagant narratives remains a generic trait of romance novels and adventure stories early and late (Robin Hood, Hercules, Xena the Warrior Princess, Indiana Jones), but, at least for earlier audiences, it makes *Adam Bell* a story of national significance.

This conflation continues throughout history, with legends growing around factual outlaws: Jesse James, Billy the Kid, Bonnie and Clyde, and even Pablo Escobar – all of whom were called a Robin Hood in their day.

It is now time to look at some real-life legendary figures of the Middle Ages who combine fact and fiction and who are frequently considered to have lain down the factual origins for the Robin Hood legends.

Chapter Four - CONTENDERS

Many possible contenders for either the real-life Robin Hood or the real-life inspiration behind the legend's origins have been identified by historians. Some are serious possibilities; others less so. But one needs to be aware that some of those at the top of the list are usually more likely to have contributed to the developing folklore rather than to have initiated it.

The historical figures discussed in these final two chapters are all real, flesh-and-blood, documented figures. The crucial fact they have in common is that they were all active by the mid-thirteenth century. This is because, as discussed in chapter two, the Berkshire evidence from 1261-62 reveals that the legend of Robin Hood was known by this time; this therefore precludes any figures from after this time as having contributed to the origins of the tales. They may have helped develop the legend, but they are not its source. The other issue very much to the fore in these final chapters is constant awareness of the central hero / outlaw paradox: do these contenders resolve this paradox? And if so, how and why?

The three historical figures that follow in this chapter are arranged in ascending order of probability, with another in the final chapter being a previously completely overlooked contender by other historians, but whom I consider the most qualified candidate by far as the being central in the formulation of the Robin Hood legend. In the previous chapter, we looked at how fact and fiction merged in medieval criminal tales. Our first three subjects, all identified as possible Robin hoods, exemplify this.

Eustace the Monk

Eustace is one of the most colourful characters of the entire Middle Ages. A flavour of his life can be summed up by the title of a popular talk I regularly give on him and of a forthcoming book I am writing: *Eustace the Farting, Foul-Mouthed, Cross-Dressing Monk and Notorious Medieval Pirate*. But even this does not do him justice.

Eustace was active between circa 1190 and 1217, during which time he developed an international reputation. As Keen says of him: "We know more of the life of the historical Eustace than we do of any of the other outlaws, for of all of them, it was he who made the deepest impression on the history of the times". He is often known as "the Robin Hood of the Seas" because of his career as a pirate; but, as we are about to see, most of the tales about him are actually set during his time as a bandit operating in the woods.

Eustace features in administrative and chronicle records of the time; the contemporary writer Anonymous of Béthune, who may have met Eustace, says of him: "No one would believe the marvels he accomplished or which happened to him on many occasions." Burgess, who has provided an excellent modern text of the tale, says of this comment: "However frightening a figure Eustace was, there is surely a strong element of admiration in these words." Most of these marvels – real or imaginary – are set down in a whole tale devoted to his life: *The Romance of Eustace the Monk*. It was written in Old French sometime between 1223 and 1284; it preserved his reputation for modern audiences but was written to reflect the reality that Eustace had become a legend in his own lifetime.

Eustace was born circa 1170 near the seaport of Boulogne. Although he trained as a knight, the lure of the sea was too strong for him. The *Romance* – our chief and greatly embellished source for his early years – says he went to Toledo in Spain to school himself in the art of necromancy. He also schooled himself in the craft of seamanship during his travels around the Mediterranean. But on his return to France he entered a monastery around the year 1190: a perplexing and disastrous career choice. Eustace was not, to put it mildly, suitable for the reflective life of the cloisters; he must have been one of the worst monks ever to have taken the habit.

Hardly had he been tonsured when he was causing mayhem, performing "many devilish acts". (All following quotes are from the *Romance*, until stated otherwise.) He urged the brothers to eat instead of fast, to curse when they should have been reciting the holy office, and the peace of the cloister was disturbed by the farting that Eustace encouraged. No wonder his abbot exclaimed in despair: "This man is a demon!" Unsurprisingly, before long Eustace left – or was ejected from – the monastery.

Eustace managed to find himself an influential new position as comital seneschal (main administrative officer) to Count Renaud of Boulogne, a powerful figure in France. He is to become the Sheriff to Eustace's Robin. The two fall out, partly because Eustace seeks revenge for the count's failure to provide justice for the murder of his father, and partly because Eustace is defrauding the count through financial misdeeds. Eustace takes to the forest to escape and embarks on his new career of banditry. It is on this aspect of the Eustace's life and his battles with the count, against whom Eustace swears vengeance, that the *Romance* focuses and where the legend becomes fully formed.

Eustace and his men rob, plunder and have narrow escapes – all elements familiar to readers of Robin Hood. But there are even stronger similarities. Eustace loves to dress up in disguise to trick the count, on one occasion as a potter, another as a leper and another as a one-legged beggar with one of his legs bound up, who escapes by leaping up on to one of the count's horses and riding off "with his crutch hanging down". On another occasion he dresses up as a woman (or prostitute) and pretends to seduce a randy young knight: "Let me get on this horse and I will give you a fuck." The knight is prepared to pay for services he expects to be rendered, with Eustace cheekily telling him that "I will teach you how to use your bum". As the knight lifts Eustace's leg, Eustace lets out an enormous fart and blames this on the sound of the horse's leather saddle. The knight is tricked and Eustace rides off on the stolen horse.

Then there is the darker side, so beloved of medieval outlaw tales. Eustace captures five of the count's knights and cuts off the feet of four of them; the fifth "does not forget the trotters". And, in an episode recalling the page in "Robin Hood and the Monk", Eustace seizes a young boy spying for the count and forces him to hang himself, without even having the opportunity to make his confession. The *Romance* writes that Eustace "knew so much about evil and guile".

Eustace's later career – as a highly effective admiral – is hardly less dramatic and is more factually documented. At first Eustace serves with John, is rewarded with a mansion, and sets up a pirate base in the Channel Islands. But he changes sides to the French when, according to the *Romance*, John took Eustace's wife hostage and disfigures, burns and kills his daughter. John's alliance with Count Renaud is probably the real cause of this change of allegiance. King Philip of France is delighted to welcome Eustace:

> You are not big, but small, yet you are so brave and bold. You know a great deal about guile and cunning and do not

need a cat's grease to help you [ie, you are slippery and crafty enough]. Thereafter, the monk was a good warrior.

He serves the French well until his capture by the English at the naval battle of Sandwich in 1217. (Although this part of his life is documented historically and is truly dramatic – as I show in my book *Blood Cries Afar* – the *Romance* loses interest when Eustace leaves the greenwood for the high seas, and wraps up the story somewhat abruptly with the focus on Eustace's end.) When the English board his ship "the brave and courageous" Eustace violently swings an oar about him, knocking the enemy to the ground. But when the ship is overrun, he hides in the ship's hold. He is found, dragged up to deck and beheaded. The last line of the tale reads: "No one intent on evil can live for a long time". His head was stuck on a pole and paraded around England's southern ports to reassure people that this terror of the seas is dead.

So there is plenty here to compare with the Robin Hood legend. As well as the historical timing there is comedy, trickery, disguises, the central role of the forest, violence, an authority figure as the chief foe and joining the service of a king (or two). But it is very important to recognise with Eustace and in the tales below that these similarities present standard literary devices and vehicles for outlaw tales: it is not that these tales conform to the Robin Hood template, but that the Robin Hood legend conforms to a much larger and more widespread one.

Despite his popularity among some writers as a Robin Hood figure, Eustace does not convince on a number of accounts. He is of knightly class, not yeomanry stock. He has no significant association with the bow. Very tellingly, he is not English, at a time when patriotic national identity was growing in the country; England was at constant war with France, so a French hero would be beyond the pale and likely to get a minstrel or ballad singer strung up rather than applauded. And, despite some grudging respect afforded to Eustace, he is an "evil" man who cannot reconcile the hero / outlaw paradox.

At best, then, Eustace may offer some inspiration for a Friar Tuck type figure and the general tale of outlawry may well have contributed to the outlaw fiction and song genre. But a French bandit knight is not an English yeomanry hero.

Fulk Fitzwarine

With Fulk Fitzwarine (variously spelt Fouke Fitz Waryn, Fulk fitz Warin, etc) we have a knight that gains legendary status. As Painter summarised many years ago:

> The whole affair is extremely curious. A simple knight of meagre landed power defies the king, rises in revolt, gathers a band outlaws, and wanders about the realm for three years. Then he is pardoned [...] given what he originally wanted, and later allowed to marry a rich widow.

His tale as an outlaw is told in the Anglo-Norman prose *The Romance of Fulk Fitzwarine*, considered to be an early fourteenth-century version of a late thirteenth century poem. A version in Middle English exists; as Kelly notes: "The existence of a vernacular version of the romance not only would attest to its popularity but would increase the odds that it was known by the yeoman minstrels of the Robin Hood tradition." The adapter of the first surviving manuscript expresses strong anti-royalist sentiment against Edward II; that the story is set in the reign of King John makes it especially easy to transfer these well-founded feelings.

Fulk Fitzwarine III, a knight of the Welsh March, succeeded his father in 1197. He was involved in a dispute over the ancestral manor of Whittington; but John awarded it to the Welshman, Meurig of Powys. This drove Fulk into rebellion against John for the period 1200-03. Fulk's band comprised of fifty-two men, including brothers, tenants and sons of local prominent Shropshire families. John felt sufficiently threatened to send Hubert de Burgh with 100 knights to deal with the problem. Fulk was pardoned in November 1203 and, having paid 200 marks, was granted possession of Whittington castle a year later.

The *Romance* is based on this period of Fulk's life. Just as with the tale of Eustace, the writer loses interest for the rest of his subject's long career, devoting only five per cent of the whole to this, despite the fact that Fulk lived on until 1258. He served with the king before joining the 1215 Magna Carta rebellion. Thereafter he remained involved with Anglo-Welsh politics until his death. Thus, again, it is the time of banditry that holds the literary appeal.

The first third of the *Romance* takes the Fitzwarine story back to King William the Bastard's time in the eleventh century. This is done so as to show the justice of Fulk's claim on his lands. This is no straight genealogical account: in the first few pages the foundation myth of Brutus is recounted; a knight fights a mace-wielding, fire-breathing devil; and King William takes possession of the Devil's club. There are also tournaments, one-on-one combats in battles, heraldry and other clearly chivalric elements relayed; there are "bold and proud" knights aplenty.

The main story then concentrates on the conflict between Fulk and John. The author delights in painting a bad picture of John "who all his life was wicked, argumentative and spiteful [...] He is without a conscience, is evil, angry and hated by everyone". Fulk, in the tale, is raised in the royal court, friends of Henry II's sons Henry, Richard and Geoffrey, but at odds with Prince John. When the young John throws a chessboard at Fulk and hurts him, we are to believe that Fulk kicked the royal prince so hard in the chest he blacked out. John never forgave him and the seeds of their dispute were thus sown.

When John becomes king, the consequences are played out, with John taking his revenge by awarding Whittington to Meurig (Morys). Fulk renounces his homage to John and begins his opposition. Fulk and his brothers overcome a much larger force of knights sent to apprehend them, but these are easily defeated ("some lost their noses, others their chins"), and Fulk gathers his forces in Babbins Wood (the *Romance* claims he also had an army of "500 footsoldiers"). However, Fulk's force moves around: when an army of 100 knights attempts to hunt him down, he and his army search "through all of England". This force "feared Fulk's noble chivalry […] and his strength and bravery". More realistically than in the fairly static Robin Hood tales, Fulk moves over 120 miles south into Braydon Forest in Wiltshire, where he waylays merchants of the king; he releases them after giving them a hearty dinner. He shares the spoils equally among his men. Fulk and his men never harm anyone "except the king and his knights". All these are familiar elements in Robin Hood.

The tale continues in this vein. Fulk is pursued by large forces; there are numerous combats and fatalities; one of Fulk's men uses a crossbow to kill an opponent; Fulk disguises himself as a monk and as a merchant; he tricks other knights; a knight plays the part of a minstrel to rescue a comrade; there is more violence over chess. At one point Fulk shoes his horse backwards to throw off the pursuit of his enemies, a trick deployed in Eustace's tale and in Hereward's (see below). The story then turns truly fanciful again with Fulk's adventures off the coast of Scotland and as far afield as the Nordic countries. These see him rescuing seven damsels, slaying dragons and encountering "a venomous beast with the head of a dog, a thick bead like a goat and ears like a hare"; thence to Spain where he rescues another damsel from a dragon. He returns to England and disguises himself as a charcoal burner to fool John, whom he captures and releases on oath. Fulk squares off against the king's forces with more graphic violence ("cut through to his heart and lungs") and escapes again. In quite a location shift, he finds himself encountering the King of Barbary and another fantastical adventure resulting in Fulk marrying the king's sister, who recognises that he is a man of "truly courtly bearing". He returns once more to England where he captures King John in the New Forest. This time John holds to his word and Fulk has his lands reinstated.

Amidst all this there is the expected dark humour as when Fulk slays twenty opponents: "Fulk had that many fewer enemies!" And extreme violence: at one point he makes a prisoner cut off the heads of bound prisoners before Fulk dishes out the same treatment to him. Elsewhere, six haughty peasants get above their position so Fulk decapitates them all.

So the tale shares with Robin's those stock devices of trickery, disguise, violence, fighting for justice, hiding in forests, dinner for those robbed, helping ladies, robbing the king's men, close escapes, ambushing his knights, righteous violence in revenge or in self-defence, sharing the loot fairly among his followers – and much more besides. The timing is perfect, too, for the origins of the Robin Hood legend. So there is much to be said for those seeing Fulk as a leading contender.

However, while a better candidate than Eustace, Fulk is not convincing in the role, either. The main argument is that the *Romance* is so wholly chivalric in tone: written about knights to be read and heard by knights. All the elements of traditional chivalry are here: rescuing damsels, heroism in mounted combat, heraldry. Disputes are over land, not money and loans. There are no concerns over yeomanry status, only knightly status and honour. Indeed, when Fulk encounters the six peasants taking on airs and graces, he kills all the "scoundrels".

As Bedford notes: "The typos of outlaw as bringer of justice could not provide the same kind of authoritative precedent to an audience as could the chivalric hero", which is exactly what Fulk is. Also notable is that Fulk is in open military rebellion against a cruel king; there is no respect there. Nor is there a bow to be found, either. And the first Robin Hood tales, though sometimes implausible, do not include the incongruous fantasy elements that feature so heavily in Fulk's fictionalised life story. So Fulk Fitzwarine goes some way to resolve the hero / outlaw paradox and fits the time, but he belongs to a different class and is intended for a different audience. He is not an everyman hero. Again, that is not to say that Fulk's story did not influence Robin's; but both employ the usual literary tropes common to the outlaw genre. Robin's origins are to be sought elsewhere.

Hereward the Wake

The legend of Hereward shares the fantastical element present with Fulk. However, with Hereward we have, in an indirect way, the strongest of all contenders for the real-life origins a Robin Hood-style legend – before my new identification of a later Hereward counterpart, whom we discuss in the final chapter. Hereward was a minor Anglo-Saxon (ie, English) landholder with ancestral domains in Lincolnshire, who resisted the Norman conquest. Nobility aside, we see in his tale preserved for posterity many direct parallels with the Robin Hood stories, suggesting an early presentation of stock literary motifs in medieval outlaw tales.

A genuine historical figure, we know little of Hereward's life, despite his presence in the *Anglo-Saxon Chronicle* and other contemporary sources, as well as later ones such as by Roger of Wendover. Before 1066 he was exiled, perhaps on the wishes of his father. Following the Norman Conquest of England starting in 1066, Hereward's lands were granted to the new Norman rulers. This by itself is a solid reason for his taking up banditry in the Fenlands of eastern England. He allied with the Danish King Sweyn during the latter's invasion of the north of England in 1070, presumably following the thinking that my enemy's enemy is my friend. Hereward becomes a symbol of English resistance, not least for his long stand against William at Ely between 1070 and 1071. For this resistance, Hereward became a national champion.

His story is told in the *Gesta Herwardi* (the *Deeds of Hereward*). The earliest extant manuscript is from the thirteenth century. There are strong indications that the original may have been written in the early twelfth century by someone who heard first-hand testimony. As Bradbury has described it, it is "probably a twelfth-century work about this eleventh-century hero found in a thirteenth-century collection of legal documents". As with Fulk's tale, it mixes fact, embellished fact and fantasy. As with all such outlaw stories, it is heavily romanticised.

The lack of information about Hereward's youth is not a major problem for the writer: he simply makes up fairy stories of the sort that appear later in Fulk's tale. The saga begins with Hereward being exiled from the country and earning the name of "Outlaw". On his travels he kills a giant Norwegian bear "which had the head and feet of a man and human intelligence", slays a tyrant and disguises himself to kill someone else. In Flanders he credibly fights to gain an impressive military reputation. Returning to England, "now subject to the rule of foreigners", he avenges the killing of his brother by the conquerors, who had seized the family manor at Bourne. Taking his brother's head impaled on a gate post "he kissed it and concealed it and wrapped it in cloth". Confronting the drunken Normans who were "abusing the English race" through their mockery, he slaughters all fifteen of them and, in turn, hangs their heads over the gate. At Peterborough he is knighted "in the English tradition" (a part of the tale that belies its later medieval origins). Killing the brother of one of King William's most import barons, Hereward again heads to Flanders to perform more martial deeds of renown.

His next return to England marks the beginning of his organised resistance to Norman rule; the *silvatici* emerge from the forests to take a stand. The final two-thirds of the *Deeds* is taken up with Hereward's defence of Ely and its immediate aftermath. As Bennett writes: "Ely seems to have become a beacon of resistance as much as a last refuge". Here the outlaw hero transforms into a true national hero, battling against the Norman occupiers and oppressors. At Ely Hereward is warmly welcomed by "important men", leading English figures (some of whom might not actually have been there), thereby showing the respect Hereward receives from social superiors.

As King William launces a massive siege operation to crush this last remnant of English defiance, the tale combines authentic details of the lengthy investiture embroidered with unlikely events to showcase Hereward's bravery and ingenuity. Before Eustace, and before Robin Hood, Hereward takes on the disguise of a potter to spy on the king's court; he is captured and escapes. In his next disguise as a fisherman he again causes havoc among the enemy. There is room for black humour: during the siege, a witch performing moonies from an elevated position falls and breaks her neck.

Hereward then hears that the powerful church leaders in Ely, including the abbot, have come to terms with William in order to preserve their ecclesiastical and abbatial lands. Feeling betrayed, Hereward withdraws first to a marshy camp (somewhat like Alfred the Great in Athelney, it is worth pointing out). The resources of William's kingdom, deployed at the siege, are diverted to hunt down Hereward "searching for him everywhere in the forests near Peterborough". Among these is Abbot Turold of Peterborough, a genuinely despotic churchman deserving of Hereward's – and the reader's – enmity. Again, we are treated to an early example of what becomes a stock trick in outlaw tales: Hereward shoes his horse backwards to confuse his pursuers. Hereward's men organise their defences: "They concealed all their archers and slingmen positioned in the tress, standing unseen among the branches." The abbot is captured but released for a large ransom.

The duplicitous abbot resumes his hunt for Hereward, prompting Hereward to lay waste to Peterborough and plunder the church's wealth, which a remorseful Hereward returns. There is more humour when an enemy flees Hereward and hides in a latrine, "putting his head through a lavatory seat" to beg for mercy. More individual combats follow, with Hereward always the victor, of course. Eventually, Hereward is imprisoned for a year, rescued when he is being transported through a forest, and is reconciled with the "revered" king and received into his favour, winning his lands back. (In reality, Hereward escaped from Ely and is not heard of again.)

There are too many parallels here with the Robin Hood story

to be dismissed: tricks, forests, ambushes, disguises (including as a potter), vengeance, escapes, enmity towards monastic figures, bows, violence, dark humour and reconciliation with the king, etc. Swanton rightly observes that the attitudes, weaponry and "in general the story [are] presented in terms that were likely to appeal to a rustic rather than a courtly audience". And crucially, Hereward perfectly resolves the hero / outlaw paradox. Dalton sums up the general historical consensus that Hereward is "a forerunner of the greatest outlaw of popular English mythology, Robin Hood". Little wonder, then, that Hereward should lead the field for the Robin Hood origin stories.

But there is another, more fundamental, reason, for his importance, one accurately emphasised by Hayward in 1988: that of Hereward's patriotic symbolism. This is a vital element in the case I make for the last of the contenders in the final chapter: a true historical figure who, arguably more than any other, comes closest to being not only the real-life inspiration for the burgeoning of the Robin Hood legend, but who certainly comes closest to bringing the hero of literature to life in person. And he is someone who only a handful of historians know of, and who no one has connected to the Robin Hood character before. It is time to meet William of Kensham.

Chapter Five - AN UNSUNG HERO

Eustace the Monk, Fulk Fitzwarine and Hereward the Wake are all significant figures, mentioned in the chronicles; but their real fame is owed to popular literary versions of their lives in the heroic, romantic tradition. But what if the most important real-life character in the Robin Hood story has not received the same literary treatment from medieval writers and minstrels? Or, just as likely, he did – but there are no surviving manuscripts to tell his tale? After all, the earliest Robin Hood ballads survive only from the mid-fifteenth century, even though his legend was known two centuries earlier. When was the Robin Hood legend first committed to parchment? Short of a miraculous discovery, we will never know. This final chapter examines just such a person without cultural representation, for whom we know of no literary treatment or ballads devoted to him – a true unsung hero.

But before we get to him, we must first discuss another contender in this known-but-unsung category, one who has received a good deal of recent attention with considerable reason: Roger Godberd.

Roger Godberd

Godberd was an outlaw of the mid-thirteenth century, whose criminal career is attested to in official records. He has been known as contender of sorts for a while, but his case was made most fully in David Baldwin's *Robin Hood: The English Outlaw Unmasked* from 2011. The contemporary context of Godberd's activity is one I think is both important and very relevant to the Robin Hood myth.

Godberd held lands in north-west Leicestershire from the earl of Derby, Robert de Ferrers. His life-span has been estimated as being from the early 1230s to the early 1290s. He had a notable connection with Nottingham, being a member of its garrison sometime between the late 1250s and 1264, and a prisoner there later. During the bitter civil war in England between 1264 and 1265/7, Godberd was on the side of the defeated barons rebelling against the rule of Henry III. Their leader, Simon de Montfort, was killed and his body hacked to pieces at the battle of Evesham in 1265, and it seems that from 1267 Godberd was active once again in a subsequent guerrilla movement against the forces of the crown in Nottinghamshire, Leicestershire and Derbyshire, while sustaining himself through banditry. (There are strong echoes here of Jesse James in the aftermath of the Confederacy's defeat in the American Civil War.) He made enough of an impact for the king to write to the constable of Nottingham expressing his concerns, which included "outlaws, robbers, thieves and malefactors, mounted and on foot". So many "great homicides and robberies" were carried out that "no one with a small company and no religious person could pass through these parts without being seized and killed or robbed of their goods". Even before his rebellion he was causing trouble. In 1266 the government's close rolls records show that he forced the monastery of Garendon to hand over bonds of his debts to them. A large band of rebels operated close by to Godberd; it took a government force of eighty men to defeat them in 1267.

Baldwin summarises Godberd's activities:

By 1270 he was leading a band of outlaws whose depredations ranged across several counties into Wiltshire [in the south] […] He was accused of being responsible for many burglaries, murders, arsons and robberies committed in Leicestershire, Nottinghamshire and Wiltshire, his worst being an attack on Stanley Abbey (Wiltshire) on 29 September during which he had stolen a large sum of money together with horses and valuables and killed one of the monks.

Godberd protested his innocence. The king ordered his capture which occurred in Hereford by early 1272. He and his right-hand man, Walter Devyas (a thief who had also killed a chaplain's son) ended up imprisoned in Nottingham Castle. Devyas was executed but Godberd was eventually released. Things go quiet until 1287 when justices judging criminal cases in Sherwood encounter Godberd, who has been accused of poaching. For Baldwin, Godberd and Devyas are the real Robin Hood and Little John.

There is much to commend this theory. As we have seen earlier, the Scottish chronicler Walter Bower placed the Robin Hood stories in the aftermath of the civil war. (War is, I argue in the next sections, probably the single most important factor in the Robin Hood legend.) There is conflict with monks. The links to Nottingham and Sherwood are there; but, as I make clear in chapter two, the question of this area as being the setting for the original Robin Hood tales is deeply problematic.

The counter-arguments are too strong, though. There is little of the hero about Godberd, although the De Montfortian political cause was a genuine one which attracted great popular support; but Godberd comes across as a criminal figure without redeeming features. There is no bow. The hero / outlaw paradox cannot be resolved here. And the post 1261-62 timing is wrong. Baldwin is aware of much of this. But he is right when he says that Montfort "and his associates had made enough of an impression for some of their deeds to pass into legend and become an integral part of the ballads".

Given the nature of adapting and updating the Robin Hood legend for new audiences, it is therefore very possible that Godberd did add to the development of the legend, especially the Nottingham and Sherwood connection. But there is someone else from half-a-century earlier who fits the profile more completely than anyone else, who suits the timing perfectly, and who resolves perfectly the hero / outlaw paradox.

William of Kensham: The Unsung Hero

William of Kensham is a little-known historical figure who features in early-thirteenth century English records and makes a notable appearance in the key chronicles of the time as a forest-dwelling, bow-wielding outlaw and freedom fighter. His surname is sometimes rendered as Cassingham, Collingham or Colingeham. A non-noble, minor servant of the crown, his most senior role (which was not a very elevated one) was as warden of the Seven Hundreds of the Weald in Kent, in which Kensham was a manor, lying between Sandhurst and Rolvenden. This was his reward for heroic services to the king, whom he served loyally and to great effect. We know nothing of his background prior to 1216 except that he moved into this area, wed and had a daughter and son; his land passed on first to his son, Ralph, and then to Ralph's sons-in-law.

The chronicler Roger of Wendover, whose early-thirteenth century work *The Flowers of History* is the single most important chronicle source for this period of English history, said that William was a young man in 1216, the year that he came to prominence; he was probably in his early twenties. After 1217, by which time William had established his reputation but was no longer needed in his heroic mode, his name crops up regularly in official rolls until 1251, as he was on the king's payroll in his official capacity. During this time he lived a contrasting life, occupied with regular and mundane work which included temporary law-keeping duties and supplying logs to friends of King Henry III. From the records we can deduce that he probably died in 1257, as that year his wife came under the protection of the king. (His time span coincides exactly with that of Fulk Fitzwarine, who fought on the opposite side, against the king, in the wars of this time.)

William came to fame during a time of acute national trauma. The French invasion and occupation of England between 1216 and 1217 was the greatest crisis faced by the country since the Norman Conquest in 1066; exactly 150 years on since then, history came close to repeating itself. But despite the chronicles of the age naturally being preoccupied by the massive event, the invasion itself has been barely studied. (It was while writing the first book and detailed study of the invasion, *Blood Cries Afar*, that I had my initial encounter with William.) By 1215 England was in a state of civil war, as many barons joined a revolt against the king that led to Magna Carta. To rid themselves of King John's arbitrary and increasingly despotic rule, they offered the crown to the Capetian Prince Louis of France, heir to the French throne. He landed with his army in May 1216. Before long, John was cowering in the west country while Louis ruled up to half of England, from Winchester in the south up to Lincoln in the north. He set up his headquarters in London.

The measure of Louis's success can be gauged by the fact that at one point over two-thirds of the barons in England deserted John for Louis. In the autumn of 1216 King Alexander of Scotland was free to make his way down to Dover in the south-easternmost corner of England completely unmolested by royal forces. Just as remarkably, at Dover the

Scottish king paid homage to Louis as "king of the English". Louis was indeed *de facto* king of England. In this vast area of conquest, there were three points of loyalist resistance: Windsor Castle, Dover Castle and the great forest of the Weald in Kent and Sussex. It was in this last place that William carved out his now lost legendary status.

Today the Weald remains a heavily wooded area, but in the Middle Ages it was a huge forested region covering much of the south-eastern corner of England between London and the coast, and Hampshire's New Forest to the Kent marshes, an area of some 120 miles by thirty miles. It was an almost impossible place for the French to dominate completely. Although they took oaths of obedience from towns and the authorities of the local people, William was able to operate from the Weald for the duration of the French occupation, which lasted until September 1217 – a full eighteen months. And this is where the parallels to Robin Hood become truly striking.

Roger of Wendover, whom recent research has shown to be an even more important chronicle source than previously appreciated, writes approvingly of William. He says that Louis conquered the region

> with all its towns and fortresses; but here a young man named William, refusing to make his fealty to Louis, collected one thousand archers and took to the isolated places and forests which abounded there.

Already we have a non-noble resistance fighter, leader of a large force of bowmen (*sagittarii* in the chronicle), fighting on the side of the rightful king as they hide in the forest. From here, William laid ambushes for the French as they made their way through the forest, which they needed to do not least to reach the southern ports from London. He gained instant fame and even earned himself a nickname as his *nom de guerre*: Willikin of the Weald. (Granted, to modern ears this does not have quite the ring of Ivan the Terrible, Richard the Lionheart or something like Ungar the Storm Slayer; but this was the Middle Ages where many of the names had a different resonance than they do today.)

William had gathered an irregular army, not of knights, but of yeoman and ordinary folk who possessed their class weapon of the bow. They waged a guerrilla war to great effect. The contemporary *History of William Marshal*, even though written in Old French and a work devoted to chivalry and those of knightly status, thinks William is so notable a character that he deserves attention. The biographer exhorts his readers and listeners to "witness the deeds of Willikin of the Weald". The Anonymous of Béthune, who wrote the contemporary *History of the Dukes of Normandy and Kings of France* (also in Old French), tells us admiringly of William's "noble prowess" and how he was "feared and renowned in Louis' army". Note here the allusion to noble deeds, as in Robin Hood, even though, as the Anonymous observes, William was a "sergeant", not a knight or someone of social standing. He was so well known that even the French knew him by his nickname, the Anonymous informing us that "the French called him Willekin de Wans" (they referred to the Weald area as "Wans"; in Old French it can also be written as "Waus" and "Vauz").

Roger of Wendover tells us that William "sought out and attacked the French during the whole war and killed many thousands of them". His actions and fame earned him and his men recognition at the highest level. In September 1216 King John wrote to the resistance in the Weald, thanking them for their service to the crown. Another royal communication shows John paying William and his forces to continue the fight against the French. So this yeomanry bowman is considered not only famous and impressive enough for writers, normally preoccupied with focusing on the chivalric classes, to include him in his work; but even the king is in contact with him. No wonder Willikin became a legend in his time.

In October, King John died and was succeeded by his nine-year-old son, Henry III. The new monarch's youth meant a regent was needed; this fell to the venerable William Marshal, who continued to lead the war effort to kick the French out of England. Rarely had an English king come to the throne in such perilous circumstances. The crown remained under great threat, especially when Louis' was reinforced in the Spring and his position remained dominating.

William continued his ambushes and attacks into 1217, loyal to the new king. In the war of 1216-17, many barons and knights changed their allegiances at a dizzying rate, often more than once; but William of Kensham remained steadfast in his service throughout. In February we hear of him harassing the French making their way to the coast. Louis was attempting to reach France to organise reinforcements; but first he wanted to re-take the coastal port of Rye. To this end, he set up in the neighbouring town of Winchelsea. One of his main concerns was supplying the siege of the town; but those trying to bring provisions had to run the gauntlet of William's men in the Weald. Although the Cinque ports of the south coast had pledged their allegiance to Louis, William's continued resistance provided inspiration and hope for those who wished to oppose French rule.

Once in Winchelsea, Louis found himself trapped in. At sea, an English flotilla blockaded the harbour; on land, William cut off communications with the French in London. William prevented French reinforcements and supplies from getting through to Louis by watching the roads and destroying bridges. The French were unable to get through William's hunting grounds. As the *History of William Marshal* notes: "and then there was Willikin of the Weald who harassed them fiercely". His actions were highly effective: "Louis was so harried he felt himself in desperate straits." William's reputation was enough to put the fear of God into the French, not least because, as the *History* also says, he "was of no mind to play games, having many of them beheaded". William did not have the resources to hold prisoners; not that he would have anyway: he knew the psychological impact of terror in war. We are told that the French lost 1,000 men during this particular episode of the war. Louis finally managed to escape by sea; he was rescued when Eustace the Monk daringly broke through the naval blockade.

William is recorded in the sources as being instrumental in the war again at Dover. Louis returned in Spring, bringing with him reinforcements from France. As he approached his siege camp at Dover (the castle still held out although the town was in French hands), he could see smoke rising up from it. The Anonymous of Béthune reports that William "and many of his men" had made an attack on the French camp, killed its guards, and set fire to the building. Louis was forced to abandon disembarkation at Dover and make for Sandwich instead.

What is also notable about this attack is that William led it in conjunction with no less a figure than Oliver Fitzroy, illegitimate son of King John. Again, this reveals just how well-known and respected William had become during the war. And it shows the ruling and yeomanry classes working effectually together in a common and noble cause.

In May, William was still harrying the French, hemming them in around Hythe and Romney, as he and his archers hindered their operations in that locality. That month also saw a major defeat for the French at Lincoln. A naval defeat off Sandwich in August ended Louis' plans of total conquest and he sued for peace, leaving England the following month.

In the war's aftermath, the crown recognised William's impressive service with wardenship in the Weald and also with tenements in Essex. An estimate can be made of 120 acres of land in William's holding and his elevation to the rank of squire. He received an annual income and, on his death, his wife was granted a pension for seven years. Something of an anti-climax, maybe, but the national crisis was over. But it is the same in Fulk Fitzwarine's forty year period of quietude in his tale, and Robin Hood's twenty-two years in his. Like them, William had already made his mark.

A True Legend

If William was such a legendary figure, how is that he is so little known today? One reason is that there are no surviving ballads and tales about him: he is in the truest sense an unsung hero for us. But it is probable that tales were told of him and songs sung about his deeds, but they were not written down and, if they were, they have been lost along with so much other evidence from the Middle Ages. Few people in the south-east area of the Weald know of William today; however, some still do, aware of Willikin's name and his vague association with local history. Given the lack of written information on William, this strongly suggests an enduring oral tradition – a medium completely in keeping with the Middle Ages' main form for the transmission of tales. The other main reason is that, astonishingly, even the invasion of England in 1216-17, William's theatre of performance, is largely unknown in the present day (and hence why I wrote

Blood Cries Afar). Even as an undergraduate studying English medieval history, I attended a lecture on the end of King John's reign which passed over the invasion in one sentence.

Holt has said of the Robin Hood story that in the thirteenth century it was possible that there was "a quick generation of the legend, perhaps even beginning in Robin's lifetime". This is exactly what happened with William. Just as Robin had his sobriquet, so too did William, in Willikin of the Weald, which he gained either while actually in performance of his deeds, or at most within ten years of them as contemporary sources recording his actions prove; he did not have to wait until after his death. Willikin really did become a legend in his own lifetime.

William also resolves the Robin Hood hero /outlaw paradox better than any other contender. His patriotic resistance against the French invaders clearly marks him out as a national hero. At the same time he is a full-blown outlaw: Prince Louis ruled in the south and received homage from the population for this rule. Even King Alexander of Scotland paid homage to him from one king to another. William saw himself as a loyal servant of the true crown who was fighting a just war; but he was outside of Louis' law by refusing, unlike those living under the French prince's control, to pay homage to this new ruler of half of England.

Hereward the Wake also settles the hero / outlaw paradox fully, especially in the Robin Hood context of being a non-noble. But with Hereward there is not the same dedication to royal service, not the explicit reference to his men as being a force of archers and no evidence of Robin Hood emerging in the immediate aftermath of his deeds, having to wait at least 150 years after this – the time of the French invasion and William's rise to fame. But I believe Hereward is still of great relevance to the legend, as we shall see in a moment.

One should not make too much of Robin Hood's generosity of stealing to the rich to give to the poor, but in a significant way this can be applied to William. His band of men was drawn from the locality. As well as providing advantageous knowledge of the area, the men also had another potential advantage over the French: the clandestine support of family and friends in the region. As with the Boer War and any number of historical conflicts, this would often have enabled the guerrillas to be supplied, fed and even accommodated by the local population. It is easy to envisage the spoils plundered from French troops caught in ambush being shared out among the locals, whether to support the guerrillas' families or to keep the people of the area on their side against the French.

In chapter two, I very much played down the role of geography and the dominance of Nottingham and Sherwood in the Robin Hood legend. Remember that we have seen how the survival of the surname Robinhood is exclusively from the south. But it is actually possible to make a plausible connection between William with the setting of the Robin Hood legend. During the time of the French occupation, the royal castle at Nottingham was the regional headquarters of English forces. King John, who not only knew William but wrote to him directly, spent the last few weeks of his life campaigning in Lincolnshire and near Nottingham, and in October died at Newark Castle in Nottinghamshire. As Nottingham was a royalist stronghold close to the frontline with the French, it is inconceivable that he did not have contact with his men there, updating him on the situation and providing reports. William was fresh in John's mind, as early in September he had written to the men of the Weald to thank them for their efforts against the enemy.

As one of the leading commanders of the resistance, and one of the few actually named in the sources, William would have been known in Nottingham. The propaganda value of his exploits would have been invaluable: an ordinary man who was not only standing up to the French, but leading the fight against them. He was, after all, famous enough to be written about in three contemporary chronicles, even though he was not a knightly figure. It is not far-fetched to consider tales being told of William in the royalist centre of Nottingham and elsewhere around the country to boost the morale of the people and to inspire their resistance.

Nottingham, Barnsdale and Sherwood all lie close to Lincoln, where the French reached the limit of their northern advance. There was a great deal of military activity in this area, including a long siege of the castle in Lincoln (the French and their baronial allies had taken the town). The eastern edges of Sherwood Forest were actually closer to Lincoln than to Nottingham; royalist forces would surely have used the cover of the forest to impede French movements and communications with their Scottish and northern allies. Roger Godberd's activity in the area half-a-century later may well have reinforced Nottingham's role in the Robin Hood legend. In May 1217 Lincoln was also the site of the one major pitched battle of the entire invasion episode. This area and the south where William fought were the two main theatres of operation during the occupation. The nature of medieval warfare was such that there would have been strategic co-ordination between the forces operating in the two places. Perhaps at some point William left the south to provide military intelligence and reports to royalist commanders, even to the king, of the situation behind enemy lines.

The importance of war cannot be overestimated in the Middle Ages, yet in histories it frequently is. This is the case for the forgotten French invasion of England, even though the chronicles understandably afford this moment of grave national crisis the centre of attention for their writing of this period. Just as Hayward has rightly emphasised the English hero aspect of Hereward fighting against a foreign invader, I do the same with William of Kensham. There is a lot of misunderstanding about national identity in the Middle Ages (a subject on which I have written and taught widely), with it too often being ignored or dismissed as a phenomenon, especially before the later medieval period. This is a mistake. The same authors who write about the war in which William fought speak repeatedly of resisting the French; of fighting for ones' country ("*pro patria*"); of the French as "scum of the earth" who want to "claim England as theirs"; and of exhorting English soldiers "to defend our land from those who have come from France to take it, and thus win for ourselves the highest honour". William of Kensham, like Hereward, suits perfectly the propaganda role of patriotic English hero.

It can therefore hardly be an accident than in the early thirteenth century, at the time of another invasion and national emergency (and very real fears of invasion in the years before it actually occurred), that there was a popular resurgence of the Hereward story. The locations of his tale in the Fens became, in effect, tourist attractions, with people visiting the site of an old wooden fortification known as "Hereward's Castle". Sources attest to songs being sung about him. And Hereward became a popular name for sons.

Roger of Wendover's attention to William of Kensham – with whom the well-informed chronicler was contemporaneous – echoes his treatment of Hereward the Wake. When writing of Hereward, Roger says he and his men "took refuge in the woods […] In their lairs in the woods and waste places […] they laid a thousand secret ambushes and traps for the Normans". Keen says that Roger "might just as well have been writing of Robin Hood".

What is interesting here is that Roger, an Englishmen born and bred, makes no mention of Robin Hood comparisons. Nor do the other writers who talk about him. There is no evidence at all of the Robin Hood legend until the mid-thirteenth-century. That does not preclude the possibility of it, but the lack of mention in all the great abundance of sources for the twelfth century would indicate that the legend had yet to be born.

There is another reason for the non-appearance of the name: Robin has its origins in France and was introduced to England after the Norman Conquest. It would have taken a while to become popularised, generations after the Normans had intermarried with the English and become, in effect, English themselves, and the name accepted. It is therefore not surprising to see Robin Hood absent as a legendary figure before the mid-thirteenth century and not mentioned in reference to Hereward.

Or to William. For it is highly unlikely that the tradition of Robin Hood had started by that time. We know that it was established by 1261-62, so it had developed sometime before then. Between the Norman Conquest and the mid-thirteenth century, the single biggest event in England was the French invasion of 1216-17. It is worth highlighting the fact that all the contenders discussed here share the invasion and the Anglo-French war of the time in common: Eustace fought for the French; Fulk for the barons against the king in the lead-up to the invasion; Hereward's popularity saw a resurgence at the same time; and William fought against the French. So the timing of the emergence of the Robin Hood legend may be coincidental. But it does not look that way.

That the Robin Hood narrative emerges soon after the invasion in which the leading real-life hero is a loyal, forest dwelling, yeomanry archer and avenger against unjust rule, and who was a legend in his own lifetime, might also be coincidental. But again, it does not look that way.

I am not saying that William of Kensham is the real-life Robin Hood. But it is feasible. Nor can it be conclusively proven that the Robin Hood legend begins with him – although this is very possible and even probable. What I am saying at the very least is that he is the single most important real-life figure in the development of the Robin Hood story. Before him we have nothing. Soon after his exploits in the war, the legend has either begun or been reinvigorated – and in the form that becomes recognisable today. Further research or a lucky historical survival or finding may shed more light on a "real" Robin Hood in the future. Until then, if it ever happens, we can give a name to the best candidate for the real-life inspiration behind the Robin Hood legend. William of Kensham is our man.

SELECT BIBLIOGRAPHY

There is a vast literature on Robin Hood, ranging from high scholarship to the fantastical. Below are some key texts; it is not a comprehensive list. The focus is on more recent works, which usually accommodate the findings of earlier ones; Knight's edited volume from 1999 is very helpful as a collection of older and more recent pieces. Ohlgren's *Medieval Outlaws* is worth special mention, invaluable both for its translations of outlaw tales, including those of Eustace, Hereward and Fulk, and for its excellent accompanying commentaries (eg, by Swanton, Hahn, Kelly and Ohlgren). Also extremely useful are the primary sources and commentary on crime in Musson's volume. The work of historians named in this book can be found below, sometimes in edited collections (eg, Dalton, Phillips).

- Appleby, J and Dalton, P (eds) (2009) *Outlaws in Medieval and Early Modern England,* Ashgate
- Ayton, Andrew (1992) 'Military Service and the Development of the Robin Hood Legend in the Fourteenth Century', *Nottingham Medieval Studies* 36
- Baldwin, David (2011) *Robin Hood,* Amberley
- Bellamy, John (1985) *Robin Hood: An Historical Enquiry*, Indiana University Press
- Bradbury, Jim (2010) *Robin Hood*, Amberley
- Burgess, Glynn (2009) *Two Medieval Outlaws,* Brewer
- Crook, David (1984) "Some Further Evidence Concerning the Dating of the Origins of the Legend of Robin

Hood", *English Historical Review*, 99 (392)

- Crook, David (1988) "The Sheriff of Nottingham and Robin Hood: The Genesis of the Legend?", in P Coss and S D Lloyd (eds) *Thirteenth Century England II*, Boydell
- Given, J B (1977) *Society and Homicide in Thirteenth-Century England*, Stanford University Press
- Hahn, Thomas (ed) (2000) *Robin Hood in Popular Culture: Violence, Transgression and Justice*, Brewer
- Hayward, John (1984) "Hereward the Outlaw", *Journal of Medieval History*, 14 (4)
- Holt, J C (1989) *Robin Hood,* Thames and Hudson
- Kaufman, Alexander (ed) (2011) *British Outlaws of History and Literature: Essays on Medieval and Early Modern Figures,* McFarland
- Keen, Maurice (2000) *The Outlaws of Medieval Legend,* Routledge
- King, Andy (2003) "Bandits, Robbers and *Schalvadours*: War and Disorder in Northumberland in the Reign of Edward II" in M Prestwich, R Britnell and R Frame (eds) *Thirteenth Century England IX*, Boydell
- Knight, Stephen (1994) *Robin Hood: A Complete Study of the English Outlaw*, Blackwell
- Knight, Stephen (ed) (1999) *Robin Hood: An Anthology of Scholarship and Criticism*, Brewer
- Knight, Stephen and Ohlgren, Thomas (eds) (2000) *Robin Hood and Other Outlaw Tales*, Western Michigan University Press
- Knight, Stephen (2009) *Robin Hood: A Mythic Biography,* Cornell University Press
- Knight, Stephen (2015) *Reading Robin Hood: Content, Form and Reception in the Outlaw Myth*, Manchester University Press

- Lyth, P (2006), 'Selling history in age of industrial decline: heritage tourism in Robin Hood county', *XIV International Economic History Congress, Helsinki*, 21-25 August, 2006
- McGlynn, Sean (2008) *By Sword and Fire: Cruelty and Atrocity in Medieval Warfare*, Weidenfeld and Nicolson
- McGlynn, Sean (2012) 'Eustace the Monk', *Medieval Warfare* 2 (6)
- McGlynn, Sean (2013) 'The Real Robin Hood', *History Today* 63 (3)
- McGlynn, Sean (2014) 'William of Kensham: Hero of the Resistance', *Medieval Warfare* 3 (6)
- McGlynn, Sean (2015*) Blood Cries Afar: The Magna Carta War and the Invasion of England, 1215-1217*, 2nd edn, History Press
- McGlynn, Sean (2015) *Kill Them All: Cathars and Carnage in the Albigensian Crusade*, 2nd edn, History Press
- McGlynn, Sean (2016) 'The Devil's Monk', *BBC History Magazine*, (September)
- Melrose, Robin (2017) *Warriors and Wilderness in Medieval Britain: From Arthur and Beowulf to Sir Gawain and Robin Hood*, McFarland
- Musson, Anthony with Powell, Edward (trans and ed) (2009*) Crime, Law and Society in the Later Middle Ages*, Manchester University Press
- Ohlgren, Thomas (ed) (1998) *Medieval Outlaws: Ten Tales in Modern English,* History Press
- Phillips, Helen (ed) (2008) *Bandit Territories: British Outlaws and their Traditions*, University of Wales Press
- Pollard A J (2004) *Imagining Robin Hood,* Routledge
- Prestwich, Michael (1992) "Gilbert de Middleton and the Attack on the Cardinals, 1317" in Timothy Reuter (ed),

Warriors and Churchmen in the High Middle Ages, Hambledon
- Rex, Peter (2013) *Hereward,* Amberley
- Storer, Ian (2018) "Murderers and Merry Men", *History Today* 68 (6)
- The Robin Hood Project - http://d.lib.rochester.edu/robin-hood

*

Made in the USA
Middletown, DE
03 February 2019